Natural
Wonders
of

Southern
California

Natural
Wonders
— *of* —
Southern
California

A Guide to
Parks, Preserves
& Wild Places

Anne Z. Cooke

Illustrated by Lois Leonard Stock

Country Roads Press
CASTINE • MAINE

Natural Wonders of Southern California

Published by Country Roads Press
P.O. Box 286, Lower Main Street
Castine, Maine 04421

Text and cover design by Studio 3.
Cover photograph by Doug Wilson.
Illustrations by Lois Leonard Stock.
Typesetting by Typeworks.

ISBN 1-56626-115-5

Library of Congress Cataloging-in-Publication Data

Cooke, Anne Z.
 Natural wonders of Southern California : a guide to parks, preserves
and wild places / Anne Z. Cooke ; illustrator, Lois Stock.
  p. cm.
 Cover title: The Country Roads Press guide to the natural wonders of
Southern California.
 Includes index.
 ISBN 1-56626-115-5 : $9.95
 1. California, Southern – Guidebooks. 2. Natural areas – California,
Southern – Guidebooks. 3. Natural history – California, Southern –
Guidebooks. 4. Parks – California, Southern – Guidebooks. 5. Botanical
gardens – California,   Southern – Guidebooks.   I. Haggerty, Steve.
II. Title. III. Title : Country Roads Press guide to the natural wonders
of Southern California.
F867.C72 1994
917.94″90453 – dc20   94-19459
                                                                CIP

Printed in the United States of America.
10 9 8 7 6 5 4 3 2 1

*For my father and mother,
Henry and Elsa Oldberg Zettelman,
who showed me the mountains*

Contents

Introduction

There's almost nothing you can say about California that everyone agrees with, beyond the usual superlatives about the state's huge size, dramatic scenery, and diversity of climate and geographical features. Ask any ten residents to describe Southern California's boundaries, and you'll get ten different—and spirited—answers.

In this guidebook, we've defined Southern California as the area that lies within four to five hours' driving distance of downtown Los Angeles, a region that includes ten counties (Los Angeles, Ventura, Santa Barbara, San Luis Obispo, Orange, San Diego, San Bernardino, Riverside, Imperial, and Kern) and a land area of 36,642,630 acres.

Not everyone living in this arbitrary region feels like a Southern Californian, of course. But even on the northernmost border, in Santa Barbara and San Luis Obispo Counties, most people are linked in some way and in some degree to Los Angeles by business, social, or family ties.

What everyone does agree on, however, is how much of this part of the state is still unspoiled open space. More than thirty-five percent of the total land area in Southern California belongs to protected park lands, with rugged mountain ranges, grassy inland valleys, vast desert expanses, and picturesque sandy beaches.

Within our boundaries there are four national forests, one national park, and one national recreation area. There are also 101 state parks and recreation areas, two million acres of desert, and hundreds of county and city parks.

With so much to choose from, deciding what to include in this book has been difficult. The parks we finally selected are remarkable not just for their size, quality of wilderness, or natural or historic significance, but for their recreational opportunities. Thus a 5,000-acre state park with six campgrounds and seventy miles of hiking trails might rank above a 30,000-acre wilderness that's completely inaccessible.

A road map is just the first step in finding and exploring Southern California's natural wonders. Fortunately, a host of other, more detailed maps are available from outdoor-recreation and sports stores, map stores, and auto-club offices. We suggest equipping yourself with county and road maps from an auto club, Forest Service boundary and hiking maps from national-forest ranger offices, and U.S. Geological Survey topographical maps.

A useful one-volume source for some of this information is the *Southern & Central California Atlas & Gazetteer,* an eleven-by-15.5-inch book published by DeLorme Mapping Company.

Accurate, up-to-date figures on things such as land sizes, numbers of campgrounds, miles of trails, opening dates, and prices are hard to pin down because they change so often and because, in some cases, even official statistics don't agree. Please let us know when our numbers are off.

Because of recent shortages in state and federal funds for public lands, more parks are charging parking and entrance fees, and relying on volunteers or hiring concessionaires to do the job that rangers once did. That $5 you spent to get into the state park that used to be free will help keep it open in the future.

Although we don't always support government control of open land (in Alaska, for instance, the federal government has locked up so much land that even residents can't buy a few acres), we're conservationists when it comes to California. With a population larger than Canada's and growing fast, and the resulting pressures to develop the last open land for homes, California needs its wilderness as refuge from urban sprawl.

For additional information contact the following agencies:

Bureau of Land Management, California State Office, 2800 Cottage Way, Room E-2841, Sacramento, CA 95825; 916-978-4754.

California Department of Fish and Game, 1416 9th Street, Sacramento, CA 95814; 916-653-7664.

California Department of Parks and Recreation, P.O. Box 2390, Sacramento, CA 95811; 916-445-6477.

California Deserts Tourism Association, 37-115 Palm View Road, P.O. Box 364, Rancho Mirage, CA 92270; 619-328-9256.

California State Office of Tourism, 1121 L Street, Suite 103, Sacramento, CA 95814; 800-862-2543 or 916-322-1397.

Caltrans road and weather information: 916-653-7623.

The DeLorme Mapping Company, P.O. Box 298-5500, Freeport, Maine 04032; 800-227-1656.

Disabled visitor information: 916-653-8148.

Inland Empire Tourism Council, P.O. Box 1593, Upland, CA 91785; 909-624-5651.

Los Angeles Convention & Visitors Bureau, 633 West Fifth Street, Suite 6000, Los Angeles, CA 90071; 213-624-7300.

Los Angeles County Beaches and Harbors, 310-305-9545.

Los Angeles County Parks and Recreation, 213-738-2961.

MISTIX reservations (national-forest campgrounds): 800-444-7275.

National Forests, Pacific-Southwest Region, U.S. Forest Service, 630 Sansome Street, Room 527, San Francisco, CA 94111; 415-705-2874.

National Park Service, Fort Mason, Building 201, Bay and Franklin Streets, San Francisco, CA 94123; 415-556-0560.

San Diego Convention & Visitors Bureau, 401 B Street, Suite 1400, San Diego, CA 92101; 619-696-9371.

San Luis Obispo County Visitors & Conference Bureau, 1041 Chorro Street, Suite E, San Luis Obispo, CA 93401; 805-541-8000.

Santa Barbara Conference and Visitors Bureau, 510 State Street, Santa Barbara, CA 93101; 805-966-9222.

State-park publications: 916-653-4000.

Ventura Convention & Visitors Bureau, 89-C South California Street, Ventura, CA 93001; 805-648-2075.

Ventura County Parks and Recreation, 805-654-3951.

1

Los Angeles Coastal Region

SANTA MONICA MOUNTAINS
NATIONAL RECREATION AREA

The Santa Monica Mountains may be one of Los Angeles County's smallest ranges, only fifty miles long from east to west and 3,111 feet at the top of the highest peak. But to its fans, this range is the crown jewel in Southern California's glittering panoply of public parks, a wilderness cornucopia of rocky peaks, precipitous canyons, lowland oak forests, and sandy beaches.

One of three transverse (east-west) ranges in the region, the mountains stretch from Griffith Park in downtown Los Angeles west to Point Mugu on the coast, a swath of rough and impenetrable wilderness cutting across busy and congested neighborhoods.

The range lies within 150,000-acre Santa Monica Mountains National Recreation Area, established in 1978, which unites 350 public parks and a total of 65,000 acres under a single planning and administrative umbrella. Though the region is a patchwork of public parks separated by private parcels—state beaches, county parks, and federal land alongside ranches, homes, and retreats—conservation support groups continue to buy and add new land to the park.

To sort all this out and help you decide where to go and what to do, the official SMMNRA map, available from the SMMNRA Visitors Center in Agoura, is invaluable in showing park boundaries, paved highways, dirt fire roads, hiking trails, ranches, and towns.

The park's appeal, of course—in addition to its purely scenic value—depends on its surprising recreational repertoire. Hiking, camping, backpacking, geology walks, mountain biking, horseback riding, picnicking, beachcombing, surfing, swimming, bird-watching, and kite flying—all are enhanced by the area's diverse physical features and abundant wildlife communities.

On the coast, brackish wetlands and tidepools share the water's edge with broad sand beaches. On the mountains' lower slopes, grassy valleys and tree-lined creek beds provide a safe haven for mule deer, foxes, coyotes, raccoons, bobcats, badgers, opossums, rabbits, rattlesnakes, and birds.

Along canyon-bottom creek beds, sycamores and oaks shelter wildflowers, including Indian paintbrush, Indian tobacco, wild orchids, goldenrod, prickly poppy, beardtongue, and scarlet bugler. A tangle of chaparral—a mixed community of low-water plants such as chamise, toyon, buckthorn, scrub oak, mountain mahogany, yucca, wild lilac, ceanothus, and manzanita—thrives on arid upper slopes.

Though more than two centuries have passed since the Spanish arrived in 1769, in many areas the mountains appear completely untouched, usually on former land-grant ranchos or in steep, inaccessible canyons.

You can get to various park entrances off Pacific Coast Highway (State 1), or from canyon roads that cross the mountains between Pacific Coast Highway and the Ventura Freeway. Mulholland Highway traverses the range near the summit, intersecting the canyon roads.

In the 1940s and '50s, Mulholland was a lovers' lane, a place to watch the "submarine races" at night. But today it has earned national recognition as a dramatic scenic drive, an outing well worth considering. Allow at least three hours for the trip from Griffith Park to Leo Carillo State Beach—more if you plan to take photographs.

Millions of people visit the park annually, swimming or surfing at the beach, picnicking, bird-watching, hiking, or camping overnight. School classes, scout troops, hiking clubs, and families all welcome the escape from urban sprawl.

Where: The parks within SMMNRA are accessible from exits off the Ventura Freeway, from Pacific Coast Highway between Santa Monica and Point Mugu (State 1), from a half-dozen north-south canyon roads that link the two, and from any trail or fire road crossing from adjacent city streets into the park.

Hours: Trails and fire roads are always open for hikers. Some park entrances and visitors centers are open only during the day.

Admission: Hikers are admitted free in most areas. Some state parks charge admission per car. In state-park campgrounds, sites are $14 per night in winter and $16 in summer. Phone reservations for all state-park campgrounds are essential in summer and cost an additional $6.75. Call MISTIX, 800-234-PARK.

Best time to visit: SMMNRA is accessible year-round, though many local users have their favorite months. After the spring rains, the hills are green and flowers bloom. In late summer and fall they're brown and dry. The beaches are warmest in summer, but very crowded. Many campers, fishermen, and bird-watchers prefer winter's solitude. Hiking is best in early summer, fall, and winter; summer hiking is very hot; spring is often rainy, but fresh and green.

Activities: Swimming, surfing, sunbathing, picnicking, roller skating, and kite flying are popular beach pastimes. The mountains attract bird-watchers, hikers, power joggers, and campers.

Other: All of California's beaches are open to the public. Wherever homes are built on private property at the edge of the beach, however, beachgoers are restricted to the area between the mean-high-tide line and the ocean.

Concessions: Snack bars and public bathrooms are available at most larger state beaches. Restaurants, motels, stores, and markets are strung out along State 1 on private land.

Pets: Allowed on leashes in campgrounds; not allowed on beaches or trails.

For more information:

Mountain Parks Information Line, 800-533-7275.

National Park Headquarters, 30401 Agoura Road, Agoura Hills, CA 91301; 818-597-9192.

California State Parks, 818-880-0350.

Will Rogers State Historic Park

This 186-acre property, on the edge of Topanga State Park in SMMNRA, was the home of Will Rogers, the cowboy humorist and down-home philosopher who kept Americans laughing in the 1920s with his wryly truthful remarks.

Rogers purchased the ranch, then out in the country, for his horses. After falling in love with the place (you will, too), he moved his family out of the city, building a lodge, living quarters (cowboys always slept in a separate bunkhouse), and stables in 1928. Much later, his children gave the property to the state, which maintains the house in its original condition.

Docents lead tours through the house, a Western lodge with rough open beams, pine paneling, and rustic furniture, decorated with Rogers' collection of Navajo rugs, Apache baskets, saddles, spurs, mounted game-animal heads, and a stuffed calf he used for roping practice.

Green lawns dip away from the house and up the valley, where visitors picnic and play frisbee under rows of eucalyptus trees. A regulation polo field down the hill is the site of weekend polo matches – the field was used for the match in the film *Pretty Woman*. Some of the polo ponies live in the stables, which is now an equestrian center.

Hiking maps are available in the visitors center, which doubles as Topanga State Park Headquarters. A short loop trail around the property begins behind the house, as does the eastern end of the sixty-four-mile Backbone Trail, which follows the crest of the mountains.

Where: The entrance is on Sunset Boulevard, off State 1, in Pacific Palisades.
Hours: 8:00 A.M. to 6:00 P.M. The house is open 10:00 A.M. to 5:00 P.M.
Admission: $4 per car. No fee for foot traffic.
Best time to visit: Year-round.
Activities: House tours, nature walks, trailheads leading into Topanga State Park. Polo matches on some weekends.
Concessions: The visitors center shows a short film of Rogers doing rope tricks and telling jokes. Books, trail maps, gifts, and souvenirs are for sale.
Pets: Allowed on leashes.
For more information:
Will Rogers State Historic Park, 14235 Sunset Boulevard, Pacific Palisades, CA 90272; 310-454-8212 or 818-880-0350.

Topanga State Park and State Beach

Topanga State Park—9,181 acres of beaches and mountains—is the easternmost of the three largest state parks in SMMNRA. Popular with residents of West Los Angeles, it is just west of Rustic Canyon. Elevations range from sea level to about 1,500 feet.

In summer, the beach, a mile of white sand along the coast at the foot of Topanga Canyon Boulevard, is preempted by San Fernando Valley girls (and guys) who drive over on the boulevard.

We like the park for its trails, however—especially the 4.5-mile hike at the end of Temescal Canyon. After the spring rains, the creek fills with water and flows down the canyon over the rocks, eventually reaching the ocean.

Hikers sign in near the entrance and follow the trail, which climbs the canyon's steep left side. Below, near the creek, a private campground and rustic cabins are familiar sights to folks who grew up in the area and attended summer day camp here under the sycamores and eucalyptus.

The trail continues to climb through the chaparral to the end of the lower canyon, and a waterfall and pool where children love to splash. For some hikers this is the end, but the trail crosses the stream, climbs the hills opposite, circles over the summit, and returns on the mountains' front slope.

You often see bird-watchers with binoculars at the highest point on the trail, scanning the skies for red-tailed and red-shouldered hawks, scrub jays, acorn woodpeckers, and migratory water birds. To the south and east are views of the ocean and the skyscrapers of downtown Los Angeles.

Where: Visitors centers are at Will Rogers State Historic Park and Trippett Ranch. Both have nature displays, activity schedules, and trail maps. The entrance to Trippett Ranch is on Entrada

Road east of Topanga Canyon Boulevard, eight miles south of US 101. Hiking trails enter the park at many locations around the perimeter.

Hours: Daylight.

Admission: $5 per car.

Best time to visit: Year-round.

Activities: Hiking, mountain biking on fire roads, camping.

Concessions: None.

Pets: Allowed on leashes; not allowed on most trails.

For more information:

Topanga State Park, 310-455-2465.

California State Parks, Angeles District, 818-880-0350 or 800-553-7275.

Malibu Creek State Park

For the Chumash people who lived along Malibu Creek, gathering acorns from stands of oaks in the meadows and fishing in the lagoon at the mouth of the creek, this open valley was an ideal place for a village.

No wonder, then, that after the Chumash were gone, one of the coast's most exclusive and expensive suburbs grew up on the spot. Fortunately, 6,600 acres were set aside as Malibu Creek State Park, including the beach, the lagoon, the creek and its banks, and the mountains and valleys north of the Backbone Trail.

The park, north of Malibu and south of Agoura Hills, ranges from sea level to about 2,000 feet at its crest. If many of these rocky spires look familiar to you, it's because they were the backdrop for the movie *Planet of the Apes* and for the television series "M*A*S*H," which was shot in a small valley three miles from the visitors center off Las Virgenes Road.

Fifteen miles of trails cross the park, some starting from

trailheads hear Tapia Park, off Malibu Canyon Road, and others from the visitors center. The hike to the film set is a moderate walk with some elevation gain. The trail, most of it along a dirt road, crosses several valleys and passes Century Lake, a four-acre pond created fifty years ago when the upper part of Malibu Creek was dammed. The lake is stocked for fishing.

You can recognize the "M*A*S*H" site by two completely stripped and rusted army vehicles. Mountain bikes are allowed on all these trails, although many of them are real teeth-rattlers, with rocks or sand underfoot. Since Mulholland Highway crosses the mountains just south of the visitors center, you can turn west and see some of the park by car.

The other interesting area is the lagoon and the beach, both just west of Malibu Pier. The ten-acre lagoon, created by a barrier beach, is one of the few salt-marsh habitats remaining along the coast, where a complex chain of organisms supports fish and bird populations.

On the ocean side, a long bank of rocks is exposed during

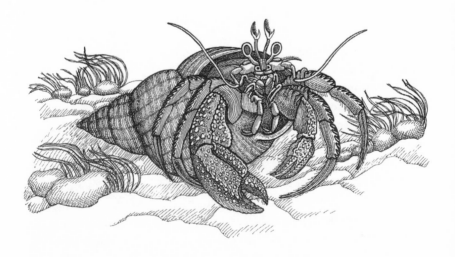

Pick up an abandoned tidepool shell and you may find a hermit crab

low tide, with hundreds of tidepools teeming with marine life. Though some of the animals are cleverly camouflaged and hard to see, the tidepools are full of sea urchins, crabs, sea anemones, sea slugs, hermit crabs, and living shells. Since the waves east of the rocks approach the beach at an angle, surfers are usually out in force. On any typical summer day, you may see photographers setting up tripods beside the lagoon, beachcombers investigating the tidepools, sunbathers catching the rays, and surfers riding the waves—all at the same time.

On the east side of the lagoon is the Adamson House, a Spanish Colonial home and former private residence of Rhoda Adamson, daughter of May Rindge. Rindge was the last owner of Malibu Rancho, the Spanish land grant that included all the land around Malibu. Tours of the house, furnished in 1930s style, are a chance to see the range of artistic ceramic tile made by the family business, Malibu Potteries. The former garage houses a museum with local-history and Native American exhibits.

Where: The entrance is four miles south of US 101 off Las Virgenes Road, just north of Mulholland Highway.
Hours: No limit.
Admission: $5 per car.
Best time to visit: Spring is greenest, but good in all seasons.
Activities: At the lagoon: surfing, tidepool exploration, swimming, and sunning. In the park: hiking, mountain biking, equestrian trails, bird-watching, camping, and nature walks.
Concessions: The campground with sixty sites, running water, and pit toilets is at the entrance station off Las Virgenes Road. The campground is rarely full, so reservations may not be necessary.
Pets: Allowed on leashes only; not allowed on trails or beaches.
For more information:
Malibu Creek State Park, 818-880-0350 or 800-533-7275.

Point Mugu State Park

A monolithic rock sticks up out of the ocean at Point Mugu on the Los Angeles County line, a perching spot for California brown pelicans and the place where the mountains sink beneath the ocean.

The rock also marks the location of 13,600-acre Point Mugu State Park, largest and most unspoiled of the SMMNRA parks, with beaches, lagoons, woodland canyons, and rocky peaks.

The park, acquired between 1966 and 1972, is a contiguous piece of land; the purchase of Circle X Ranch, on the park's eastern border in 1987, added 1,655 more acres and 3,111-foot Sandstone Peak, the highest point in the range.

The most spectacular area is along Boney Mountain, on the eastern border, where volcanic peaks thrust upward against the sky. At lower elevations, oak and sycamore woodlands in and near creek beds provide habitats for a hidden community of animals such as newts, salamanders, lizards, and tree frogs.

During one spring hike up Sycamore Canyon, soon after a rainfall, we discovered thousands of tiny toads, each about the size of a nickel, hopping along the wet sand beside the trail.

Approximately fifty miles of backcountry hiking trails start in Sycamore and La Jolla Canyons, off Pacific Coast Highway, and climb toward the crest. The Backbone Trail crosses Circle X Ranch near Sandstone Peak and enters Point Mugu State Park on the east, then continues west across Sycamore Canyon and down La Jolla Canyon to the ocean.

Two campgrounds near the ocean, in Sycamore and La Jolla Canyons, are almost always busy, and reservations are advised, especially in summer. The location is good for easy access to the beach and mountain trails. A 1,400-acre lagoon, slightly west of the park, was created by a barrier beach and nurtures a wetlands habitat.

Where: The entrance is off Pacific Coast Highway (State 1), thirty-one miles west of Santa Monica. A north entrance is on Potrero Road, south of Newbury Park.

Hours: No limit.

Admission: $5 per car for daytime use.

Best time to visit: Year-round.

Activities: Hiking, mountain biking, horseback riding, beach sports.

Concessions: A fifty-five-site campground at Big Sycamore Canyon takes tents or RVs of up to thirty-one feet. A second campground on the beach has eighty-five primitive sites.

Pets: Allowed on leashes.

For more information:

Mountain Parks Information Service, 818-880-0350 or 800-533-7275.

BEACHES NORTH OF LOS ANGELES:
Santa Monica to Oxnard

Most beaches between Santa Monica and Ventura County are public beaches, owned by city, county, or state agencies. Some are part of the California State Park system. Most are for day-time use only, with parking in public or private lots off State 1. Two state-beach parks, Leo Carrillo and Point Mugu, have campgrounds.

Each beach is different, so you have to decide whether you want to swim, surf, poke around in the tidepools, fish, or jog in splendid seclusion.

The following beaches are open for daytime use only:

Santa Monica State Beaches are wide, sandy, and wonderful for swimming. Lifeguards are on duty in the summer, and food stands and bathrooms are adjacent. Fee parking is available in public and private lots, though city residents often park free on side streets.

Will Rogers State Beach has parking and lifeguards, with limited food stands and bathrooms. Not so crowded.

Topanga State Beach, a narrow beach at the mouth of Topanga Creek, has food stands and showers.

Las Tunas State Beach, at Las Tunas Canyon, is good for swimming and bodysurfing, but has lifeguards only on summer weekends. Parking is on the street.

Las Flores State Beach is rocky and used by scuba divers; there are no bathrooms or lifeguards, and parking is on the street.

Malibu Lagoon State Beach (described in the "Malibu Creek State Park" section above) offers fantastic views, rocky tidepools, and swimming areas with limited lifeguard service. It has picnic tables and chemical toilets. Corral Canyon State Beach, a tiny beach, is nearby.

Point Dume State Reserve, along the shore at the base of the cliffs at the western end of Santa Monica Bay, is long and secluded, with hiking trails up the cliffs. Public parking is next to the beach. There are no concessions.

Zuma Beach County Park, long, broad, and sandy, is one of the biggest and best, with good swimming and great surfing, a playground, beach volleyball courts, and food concessions. There's loads of parking.

El Matador, **El Pescador**, **La Piedra**, and **Nicholas Canyon**, four small beaches at the foot of steep cliffs, are archetypal hidden coves, difficult to find and marked only by small signs on the highway. The number of visitors to these lovely coves is limited by the small parking lots atop the cliffs. Stair steps descend to the sand and tidepools. The beaches offer swimming (but no lifeguards), sunning, and opportunities for photography. There are chemical toilets in the parking lots.

The following beaches have campgrounds:

Leo Carrillo State Beach has a tree-shaded campground on the inland side of the highway, with thirty-two RV spaces and 135 tent sites. The 1.5-mile beach is expansive, wide, and sandy, with toilets, outdoor showers, and parking. The campground is great for family vacations.

Point Mugu State Park and Beach has two campgrounds with 132 sites, a developed site in the woods at the Big Sycamore Canyon park entrance, and a primitive site at La Jolla Canyon, on five-mile-long Thornhill Broome Beach. The campgrounds have water, tables, and parking. La Jolla Beach has another attraction, too: a huge sand dune that offshore winds have blown up against the cliff, an irresistible natural slide.

Where: On Pacific Coast Highway between Santa Monica and Oxnard.

Hours: Day or overnight.

Admission: $5 per vehicle fee for daytime use. Campsites, $14-$16.

Best time to visit: For the beach, summer. For hiking, fall through spring.

Activities: Swimming, bodysurfing, surfing (before 11:00 A.M. in some places), beach sports, roller skating, in-line skating, bicycling, and kite flying.

Concessions: Available in most places.

Pets: Not allowed on beaches.

For more information:

Los Angeles County Beaches and Harbors Information Service, 4701 Admiralty Way, Marina Del Rey, CA 90292; 310-305-9545.

Los Angeles County Department of Parks and Recreation, 213-738-2961.

Ventura County Department of Parks and Recreation, 805-654-3951.

ORANGE COUNTY BEACHES

Bolsa Chica and Huntington State Beaches

Bolsa Chica and Huntington State Beaches, connected by a seven-mile bike trail, provide beach access and camping for travelers driving between Los Angeles and San Diego. Both are near coastal wetlands that attract resident and migratory water birds, hence bird-watching is excellent.

Bolsa Chica State Beach, eighty-four acres in size, has three miles of flat sand and a paved parking lot for self-contained RVs and campers (no tent sites). Facilities include showers, dressing rooms, fire rings, and good wheelchair access. Across from the beach is 1,000-acre Bolsa Chica Ecological Reserve, a damaged tidal marsh that the California Department of Fish and Game has been restoring since 1973. To explore the wetlands, look for a 1.5-mile nature trail.

Huntington State Beach, with 164 acres, has fire rings for picnics and showers for swimmers, but no camping. The south end of the beach is a sanctuary for the California least tern, which nests here in May.

Where: Off Pacific Coast Highway in Huntington Beach.
Hours: Dawn to dusk, except for campers.
Admission: Fees for daytime use and camping.
Best time to visit: Year-round.
Activities: Swimming, jogging, beach sports, bird-watching.
Concessions: None.
Pets: Allowed on leashes.
For more information:
　　　Bolsa Chica State Beach, 714-846-3460.
　　　Huntington State Beach, 714-536-1454.
　　　State Park Orange Coast District Headquarters, 714-492-0802.

Crystal Cove State Park

While most beaches north of Los Angeles are public, just the opposite is true toward the south, where beach homes and private property dot the coastline. An exception is Crystal Cove State Park, near Laguna Beach on the Orange County coast, one of the last undeveloped coastal headlands.

The 2,791-acre park extends from the ocean to the head of Moro Canyon in the San Joaquin Hills, a wooded area of steep slopes and bluffs, with eighteen miles of hiking, horseback-riding, and mountain-biking trails. The tops of the hills are good vantage points for whale watching between November and March.

Four parking lots are atop the bluff, with restrooms and showers. Paths from each parking lot descend to the beach. From the Reef Point parking lot, three trails descend to the sand: a quarter-mile trail heading north goes to "3.5 Cove," a stairway descends to Scotchman's Cove, and a ramp goes south to Muddy Creek. The 3.5-mile shore is partly sand beaches and partly tidepools and rocky coves. A 1000-acre underwater park protects a particularly lush submarine environment, designed for snorkelers and scuba divers. Lifeguards are on duty between May and September.

A village built in the 1920s and now in the park has been designated a historic site. The state acquired the property and cottages from the Irvine Company in 1979 and created the park in 1982.

The park has three campgrounds, but unfortunately for car campers, they're "environmental" areas—that is, hike-in or ride-in sites located three to four miles from a trailhead. The sites have tables and "compost" toilets. You pack your water in. Horse camping is allowed at Deer Canyon campground.

Animals seen back in the canyon include coyotes, rabbits, raccoons, birds, deer, and even bobcats. Poison oak is abundant, as well. Rangers at the El Moro Visitors Center can identify it for you. Since the fall of 1993, when a forest fire burned the lower canyon, the park's inland side has been closed for restoration. Call before visiting.

Where: Off State 1 between Laguna Beach and Corona Del Mar.
Hours: Campground check-in during daylight hours.
Admission: No fees for daytime use. Fees for camping.
Best time to visit: Spring and summer.
Activities: Scuba diving, snorkeling, beach sports, hiking, mountain biking, horseback riding, camping.
Concessions: Thirty-two campsites in three hike-in campgrounds (none on the beach): Lower Moro, Upper Moro, and Deer Canyon.
Pets: Allowed on leashes.
For more information:
    Crystal Cove State Park, 8471 Pacific Coast Highway, Laguna Beach, CA 92651; 714-494-3539.

Doheny State Beach

Doheny State Beach, with sixty-two acres and a mile of sand and good swimming, is a favorite family camping place. The campground's 162 developed sites are on the east side of San Juan Creek.

    The other side of the creek is intended for daytime use, with good swimming and surfing and rocky tidepools where patient observers will find various intertidal marine organisms: starfish, sea urchins, sea cucumbers (nudibranchs), sea anemones, crabs, and mussels and other mollusks. Collecting is forbidden.

Where: Entrance off State 1 at Dana Point Harbor.
Hours: Daylight and overnight.

Admission: Fees for camping and parking; no fees for beach use.
Best time to visit: Year-round.
Activities: Swimming, jogging, beach sports, bird-watching.
Concessions: None.
Pets: Allowed on leashes.
For more information:
Doheny State Beach, 714-496-6172.
State Park Orange Coast District Headquarters, 714-492-0802.

CATALINA ISLAND

Lately when we go to Catalina, we take a helicopter from San Pedro—a sensational twelve-minute ride with aerial views of the island's rumpled peaks, canyons, and hidden coves. Last March we spied a pod of gray whales making their way toward Alaska. On another trip, the pilot caught sight of a group of buffalo, descendants of a herd that filmmakers imported years ago and eventually turned loose.

The helicopter's speed serves only to emphasize what becomes obvious after you arrive in Avalon, population 3,000, the only real town. Catalina Island, twenty-two miles across the San Pedro Channel, belongs to a simpler and more leisurely era.

Except for Avalon and a small settlement at Two Harbors, a few campgrounds, and some ranch buildings in the interior, most of Catalina's seventy-four square miles are undeveloped, thanks to its longtime owners, the Wrigley family (of Wrigley's chewing gum).

Years ago the family closed the twenty-one-mile-long island to outsiders; in the 1970s, they transferred most of their interest to the Catalina Island Conservancy, which manages it for present and future generations. The conservancy owns eighty-six percent of the island, the Wrigley family thirteen percent, and other owners one percent.

Catalina Island, the tip of an undersea mountain range, consists of the main island, with elevations to 2,097 feet, and a second small mound connected by a narrow isthmus. Most of the ragged, fifty-four-mile coast, marked by small coves accessible only by boat, is a favorite destination for weekend sailors, who anchor offshore and camp on the beach. Snorkelers and scuba divers prefer the lee (inland) side of the island because the water is warmer, calm, and clear; the water on the windward side, buffeted by the sea, is rougher and cloudier.

The vast majority of visitors dock in Avalon (arriving by boat, airplane, or helicopter) and spend their time in town window-shopping, sight-seeing, sunning on Pebbly Beach, or taking one of the guided land and water tours.

If you're willing to walk, however, a different Catalina lies beyond Avalon in the island's interior. Rocky canyons, grassy meadows, wooded mountain slopes, and secluded beaches are interrupted only by hiking trails and dirt roads. Wild goats, wild boar, foxes, deer, and ground squirrels are common, and the 300 head of buffalo are easy to spot. Several plant species are indigenous to the island.

If you're planning to camp, hike, or boat, you can bypass Avalon and go straight to Two Harbors at the isthmus. (There is one bed and breakfast here.) Boaters stop here to pick up a permit (free); hikers get their permits, as well, and either hike or ride the bus to one of four campgrounds: Black Jack (hike-in only), Two Harbors, Little Harbor, and Parsons Landing.

To avoid last-minute hitches, call for reservations. Camping fees are low and permits are free, but space is limited, especially in summer. Bus rides to campgrounds must be arranged in advance. You can't rent a car and drive through the interior.

Avalon, in fact, issues only 800 auto permits to residents,

in order to control street traffic. Most people walk, rent bicycles, or drive electric carts.

Where: Twenty-two miles from San Pedro.

Hours: No limit.

Admission: No charge to land on Avalon. Ferries, single-engine planes, and helicopters go to Catalina. Pay for tours and services on arrival. Reservations are required for some activities. The cheapest outing is to come by ferry, explore on your own, use the beach (bring your own snorkel and mask), stay for supper, and take the late ferry back.

Best time to visit: Summer is the most pleasant; late winter and early spring can be foggy.

Activities: Swimming, sunning, shopping, golfing at a nine-hole public course, hiking, backpacking, fishing, snorkeling, scuba diving; city, island, and water tours.

Concessions: The ticket kiosk for water tours (glass-bottom boats, deep-sea fishing, seal watching, whale watching, coastal cruises, sunset cruises to Two Harbors, and snorkeling) is on the pier. Land tours (scenic island, jeep safaris, city, botanical gardens, casino, and skyline drive) leave from the Ticket Kiosk in Avalon's public parking lot. Ferry services to Catalina: Catalina Channel Express, Berth 95, P.O. Box 1391, San Pedro, CA 90733, 310-519-7957 or 800-995-4385; Catalina Cruises, 320 Golden Shore, Long Beach, CA 90802, 310-491-5559.

Pets: Allowed on a leash in Avalon. Not advised.

For more information:

Santa Catalina Island Conservancy, P.O. Box 2739, Avalon, CA 90704; 310-510-1421.

Avalon Chamber of Commerce, P.O. Box 217, Avalon, CA 90704; 310-510-1520.

Los Angeles County Department of Parks and Recreation, P.O. Box 1133, Avalon, CA 90704; 310-510-0688.

Two Harbors Visitor Information and Reservation Center, P.O. Box 5044, Two Harbors, CA 90704; 310-510-2800.

GRIFFITH PARK

Griffith Park—4,107 acres of hilly, wooded terrain at the east end of the Santa Monica Mountains—is many things to many people.

To families it's the Los Angeles Zoo and Travel Town, with the largest collection of steam locomotives west of the Mississippi River. To amateur astronomers it's the observatory's "night sky" planetarium shows and science exhibits. To horseback riders it's an escape from the corral to wooded trails. To jocks it's tennis courts, golf courses, and miles of jogging trails.

But for hikers and bird-watchers, Griffith Park is an innercity refuge, a refreshing bit of mountain wilderness tucked into the concrete crook of the metropolitan freeway system.

Senior Ranger Albert Torres estimates that Griffith Park includes forty miles of fire roads and 100 miles of dedicated trails, some of which start at the "merry-go-round" parking lot near the ranger station on Crystal Springs Drive. Within a few hundred yards of asphalt and fences, you enter a forest thick enough to support healthy populations of mule deer, coyotes, foxes, skunks, raccoons, rabbits, Pacific rattlers, and king snakes.

Torres' favorite one-mile loop trail begins at the merry-go-round and winds through woods and around the old zoo property, now a refurbished park and picnic grounds, before returning to the parking lot. A longer hike is the one-way climb up 1,625-foot Mount Hollywood on the Mount Hollywood Trail, which crosses the park. To make this hike, park on Ferndell, near the intersection of Ferndell and Los Feliz Boulevard, find the trail and climb steadily for 2.5 miles to the top of the mountain. Enjoy the panoramic vistas of the Los Angeles basin, the San Fernando

A king snake

Valley, the San Gabriel Mountains, and Catalina Island, then follow the ridge downhill to Travel Town on the park's east side.

Where: The main entrance is on Los Feliz Boulevard and Riverside Drive. The visitors center and ranger station is two miles north, at 4730 Crystal Springs Drive. The park is bounded by the Foothill Freeway on the north (State 134), the Golden State Freeway (I-5) on the east, and the Ventura Freeway (US 101) on the west.

Hours: Hiking trails are open twenty-four hours. Staffed visitor attractions are open during normal business hours. The ranger station is open 6:00 A.M. to 10:00 P.M.

Admission: No charge to enter the park or hike; other attractions charge individually.

Best time to visit: Year-round.

Activities: Hiking, nature walks, jogging, tennis, golf, picnicking, family recreation.
Concessions: Available at the zoo and other attractions.
Pets: Allowed on leashes.
For more information:
   Griffith Park Visitors Center and Ranger Station, 4730 Crystal Springs Drive, Los Angeles, CA 90027; 213-665-5188.

LOS ANGELES STATE AND COUNTY ARBORETUM

E. J. "Lucky" Baldwin's Queen Anne Cottage, coyly Victorian with its white cupola and gingerbread trim, was peeking through the trees on the spring day we drove out to the 127-acre Los Angeles State and County Arboretum in Arcadia.

It had rained the day before, and the sky behind the San Gabriel Mountains was unusually blue. Around the arboretum, daffodils, tulips, lilacs, and cherry trees bloomed all shades of purple, pink, white, and yellow.

On the lagoon, ducklings paddled behind their mother, eyeing the humans and keeping a sharp lookout for airborne snacks. We disappointed them by snapping photos instead of tossing bread crumbs. Then we walked around the lake to look at the cottage.

According to arboretum historian Sandy Snider, the Queen Anne Cottage, a California Historic Landmark, "was built by Baldwin in 1885, not 1881, despite the wording on the plaque. And it wasn't built for his third wife, as most guidebooks say."

Instead, says Snider, it was intended to be a guest house for the friends and celebrities who flocked to see Rancho Santa Anita, then one of Southern California's most progressive farms.

In 1875, Baldwin, a self-made millionaire flush with real-estate and silver-mining profits, bought 8,000 acres in Rancho

Santa Anita, the 13,319-acre land grant deeded thirty years earlier to pioneer Hugo Reid.

Baldwin, who loved trees and gardens, set to work planting and nurturing a collection of native and exotic plants, many of which still grow in the arboretum. Because he was also a truck farmer, cattle rancher, and horse breeder, the rancho soon became an agricultural show place, as popular in its day as Disneyland would become some eighty years later.

Author and historian Carey McWilliams wrote that in 1885 alone, Rancho Santa Anita produced and sold 104,000 pounds of butter, 43,856 boxes of oranges and lemons, 384,460 gallons of wine, 54,946 gallons of brandy, and 174,750 sacks of grain.

But the tales of plenty told in the East and Midwest, of palm trees and orange groves, endless sun, rich soil, and cheap land, sparked a migration and land boom that doomed the ranchos. Eventually Baldwin's ranch was subdivided and sold for home lots; only 127 acres and his prize botanical collection were spared to become the heart of the city's public arboretum.

Paved and gravel paths wander through the arboretum, where seasonal flowers bloom year-round. Spring is especially lovely. Visitors can walk around the cottage's porch and look at the furnished rooms through the windows.

Where: In Arcadia, northeast of downtown Los Angeles.

Hours: Daily 9:00 A.M. to 5:00 P.M.

Admission: $3 for adults, $1.50 for seniors and students, seventy-five cents for ages six to twelve. Free on the third Tuesday of each month.

Best time to visit: Year-round. Blossoming trees and bulbs emerge in late February.

Activities: Nature walks, flower photography, identification of rare trees and plants.

Concessions: The gift shop supports the Arboretum with sales of plants, gardening books, cookbooks, and gifts.
Pets: Not allowed.
For more information:
   Los Angeles State and County Arboretum, 301 North Baldwin Avenue, Arcadia, CA 91006; 818-821-3222.

HUNTINGTON BOTANICAL GARDENS

It's hard to do justice to the 200-acre Huntington Estate in a single afternoon—the Botanical Gardens, the house with its antique treasures, and the library, a repository for thousands of priceless manuscripts and books, are a tall order for one visit.

   So if it's gardens you're looking for, before you tour the house wander through the lushly landscaped 150-acre grounds on the network of paths that connect one plant community to another.

   The Botanical Gardens, which spread out behind the house and down a hillside, were born in 1913 when Huntington decided to build a Japanese garden with an authentic teahouse and a red-lacquered bridge over a koi pond.

   Emboldened by success, he added more gardens divided by lawns, trees, paths, and, occasionally, buildings. Today there are fourteen gardens: a rose garden, a palm garden (with 200 palm varieties), a desert garden, a cactus greenhouse (for small, delicate varieties), a mausoleum garden (where the Huntingtons are buried), a formal camellia garden, a rustic camellia garden, an herb garden where plants are grouped by use (medicinal, edible, fragrant), a Shakespearean garden with plants typical of the sixteenth century, an Australian garden, a subtropical garden, a jungle garden, orange and avocado groves, and a lily pond.

Where: In San Marino, a suburb of Pasadena, northeast of downtown Los Angeles.

Hours: Tuesday–Friday 1:00 to 4:30 P.M.; Saturday and Sunday 10:30 A.M. to 4:30 P.M.; closed holidays.

Admission: Suggested donations are $5 for adults and $3 for children.

Best time to visit: Year-round.

Activities: One-hour docent tours start at 1:00 P.M. Picnics and wedding photo sessions are not allowed.

Concessions: Patio Restaurant, Tea Room. A well-stocked museum shop sells art, history, travel, children's, and gardening books, plus stationery, calendars, postcards, and gifts.

Pets: Not allowed.

For more information:

Huntington Estate, 1151 Oxford Road, San Marino, CA 91108; 818-405-2141.

2

Los Angeles and Inland

Los Angeles County, population 8,800,000, a maze of cities built back to back and connected by freeways, often looks and feels terrifyingly urban. Not so obvious, however, is the fact that nearly forty percent of the county's 2,610,730 acres belong to federal, state, county, or city agencies, much of that land within public parks—forests, mountains, canyons, valleys, marshes, and beaches—set aside for future generations to enjoy.

This chapter describes parks and wildernesses in inland Los Angeles County and in parts of San Bernardino and Riverside Counties, excluding desert areas, which are described in chapter 5.

The region is bounded by the San Gabriel and San Bernardino mountain ranges on the north, by the Riverside–San Diego county line on the south and by the Mojave Desert and the San Jacinto Mountains to the east.

The mountains: The San Gabriel and San Bernardino Mountains are the region's defining feature. Transverse ranges running east and west, they vary in elevation from 1,500 feet in the foothills to 11,499 feet at the highest point – massive barriers that divide the coastal lowlands from the Mojave Desert.

The two ranges moderate the coastal climate, blocking moist air from the ocean, and heat and cold from the desert. For this reason, palm trees thrive beside the ocean, and winter snow blankets the mountain summits.

The mountains have also determined the growth of towns and the pattern of highways. In effect, as the metropolis has spread, the mountains have become islands of wilderness dividing cities, counties, and regions.

Only three major highways – I-5, I-15, and US 101 (the coastal highway) – cross northward over low mountain passes and out of the L. A. Basin, causing the region's infamous weekend traffic jams. The problem was highlighted in January 1994, when the Northridge Earthquake closed I-5, blocking the movement of north-south traffic.

Los Angeles today: As the last bits of open space dwindle, conservation groups are redoubling efforts to find and buy the last bits of undeveloped mountains, canyons, valleys, and ranch land. But with land prices at a premium, builders and developers often have the upper hand. How the two forces divide Southern California's last remaining wild places will affect the long-term quality of life in the region.

ANGELES NATIONAL FOREST

When February skies darken over Los Angeles and gray clouds dump rain on city streets, it's a safe bet that snow is falling above 6,000 feet, frosting the rocky summits of the San Gabriel Mountains. Wet weather is a signal for Los Angeles residents to dig out coats, gloves, and sleds and head for the snowy slopes of the city's closest mountain range and the forest that surrounds it, 693,667-acre Angeles National Forest.

The forest, covering approximately one-quarter of Los Angeles County, with elevations ranging from 1,500 feet in the foothills to 10,064 feet on the summit of Mount San Antonio (better known as Mount Baldy), is one of the country's most heavily used public recreation areas.

Each year, thirty-two million people visit Angeles National Forest, driving on scenic highways, hiking on trails, camping overnight, or skiing on the upper slopes. The San Gabriels are in danger of being loved to death, but so far nothing—not crowds, not a critical shortage of federal funding, not their location astride a big city—has fundamentally altered their wild and rugged aspect or the quality of summer and winter recreation.

Cloaked in winter white, the forest looks pristine and feels primeval. Snow piles up on north-facing slopes and blows into deep canyons, dusting the needles on Jeffrey pines and incense cedars. Icicles gleam and drip in the pale winter sun, and nighttime temperatures dip to zero.

After each snowstorm, the highway department plows Angeles Crest Highway (State 2, the main east-west summit road), and cars arrive carrying families with sleds and skiers heading for the lifts at the ski areas.

In summer days are hot and nights are cool, ideal weather for hiking, mountain biking, and stargazing. Of the forest's sixty-eight campgrounds, some of the busiest are along State 2. Drive-in campgrounds are developed, with water, pit toilets, picnic tables, and grills, while most walk-in sites are primitive, often without water.

The two biggest developed recreation areas are Crystal Lake, at the end of State 39, twenty-five miles north of Azusa, and Big Pines, near Wrightwood at the eastern end of State 2. Both have lakes stocked for fishing, developed campgrounds, supply stores, and trailheads into the wilderness.

In the past, ranger-guided nature walks and campfire programs have been a traditional part of summer activities, but as funds have disappeared, rangers have cut back or relied on volunteers. To find out what's offered and when, check with local ranger districts.

A thousand miles of roads—old wagon tracks and fire roads, plus 625 miles of trails—let hikers explore most areas. Only the remote hearts of the San Gabriel and Sheep Mountain Wildernesses are truly untouched.

The Pacific Crest Trail, running 2,620 miles from the Canadian border to the Mexican border, crosses Angeles National Forest; it enters on the north near Soledad Campground (south of Vasquez Rocks County Park), traverses the high country heading east, and exits the forest north of Mount Baldy.

History: If you enter the forest at La Canada (northwest of Pasadena) and head up Angeles Crest Highway, stop at the Clear Creek Vista turnout, nine miles in, and read Historic Landmark number 117. The plaque is a reminder that forest conservation in Southern California began in 1892, when President Benjamin Harrison declared this wilderness one of the nation's first forest reserves.

It wasn't a moment too soon. Fifty years of hunting had eliminated wolves and grizzly bears, endangered black bears, and threatened deer and other wildlife. Trout streams were fished out, loggers had clearcut timber, and ranchers had burned what was left to enlarge grazing land.

As resources disappeared and soil erosion intensified, Abbott Kinney, chairman of California's first Board of Forestry (today he's usually remembered as the developer of the beach town of Venice), and others banded together to save the San Gabriels.

In 1891, Congress enacted the first Forest Reserve Act, and the San Gabriel Timberland Reserve was created the following year. In 1907, the reserve was renamed San Gabriel National Forest; a year later it became Angeles National Forest.

Angeles National Forest today: Recovered after a century, the forest is now a recreation area for city dwellers and an important watershed for four rivers: the San Gabriel, the Santa Clara, the Los Angeles, and the Mojave. At lower elevations, chaparral softens the slopes, with some digger and Coulter pines. In spring and early summer, waterfalls cascade down creekbeds, and ferns and wildflowers bloom along the banks, softening the semidesert habitat.

Above 4,000 feet, the forests are tall and thick, with a

Long-eared mule deer

mixture of ponderosa and Jeffrey pine, sugar and limber pine, Douglas fir, white fir, cedar, white and live oak, and white alder. The timberline at this latitude, varying between north- and south-facing slopes, is about 9,500 feet.

Many more animal species live in the forests than are seen. But the quiet hiker with binoculars may spot Nelson bighorn sheep, black bears, coyotes, mule deer, bobcats, raccoons, skunks, gray foxes, ground squirrels, lizards, and Pacific rattlesnakes. Dozens of birds are year-round residents.

Deer hunting is allowed in season (usually fall and early winter) in some areas. The first days of the hunting season aren't a smart time to hike. For dates and hunting areas, call the appropriate ranger district.

The biggest threat to the mountains—after man—is fire, a hazard when the forest is dry, from August through November. The threat is multiplied when warm Santa Ana winds blow from the Mojave Desert. During high-risk weeks, camping and/or campfires may be prohibited. Open fires are allowed only in designated campgrounds. Backpackers must use stoves.

Where: In northwest Los Angeles County, accessible from the Foothill Freeway or from State 14 and State 138.
Hours: No limit.
Admission: No admission.
Best time to visit: January through March for winter sports. May through September for summer sports. October, at the end of a long dry summer and before winter rains begin, is fire month.
Activities: Hiking, camping, wilderness skills, backpacking, orienteering, mountain biking (except in wilderness areas and on the Pacific Crest Trail), stargazing, nature walks, and bird-watching. In winter: skiing, snowshoeing, sledding, and snow play.
Concessions: Few and unreliable, except at ski resorts. Bring your own supplies, lunch, snacks, and hot and cold drinks.

Pets: Allowed on leashes.

For more information:

Angeles National Forest Headquarters, 701 North Santa Anita Avenue, Arcadia, CA 91006; 818-574-5200.

Saugus District, 30800 Bouquet Canyon Road, Saugus, CA 91350; 805-296-5847.

Tujunga District, 12371 North Little Tujunga Road, San Fernando, CA 91342; 818-899-1900.

Arroyo Seco District, Oak Grove Park, Flintridge, CA 91011; 818-790-1151.

Mount Baldy District, 110 North Wabash, Glendora, CA 91741; 818-335-1251.

Valyermo District, 29835 Valyermo Road, P.O. Box 15, Valyermo, CA 93563; 805-944-2187.

Angeles Crest National Scenic Byway

When out-of-state friends visit us, we always suggest a day's drive across the crest of the San Gabriel Mountains on Angeles Crest Highway (State 2). The 64-mile route, recently designated a National Scenic Byway, runs from the town of La Canada on the west to the rustic village of Wrightwood at the east end of the mountains.

Following the rocky spine of the San Gabriels across its loftiest and most spectacular heights, the road never fails to impress people surprised to find high peaks, deep canyons, and panoramic vistas so close to the city.

To the north, the Mojave Desert stretches away into the haze, and to the south, the Los Angeles Basin slopes away to the Pacific Ocean. As the road snakes upwards, climbing the sides of near-vertical canyons toward the summit's level slopes, it passes the historic sites of early lodges, pine-shaded picnic areas, campgrounds, two visitors centers, hillside waterfalls, scenic-viewpoint parking areas, and five ski resorts.

A network of hiking trails begins here at the crest, either descending into side canyons and looping back up, or climbing to mountain peaks higher than the road. The Pacific Crest Trail passes this way, as well, paralleling the crest on the north side of the road. Plan to spend a day on this jaunt. The two-lane road is in good condition, but winds back and forth, and you'll want to stop often to sightsee or take pictures.

Leave the Foothill Freeway in La Canada at the "Angeles Crest Highway" sign, and turn north past a dozen residential streets to the national forest. Nine miles from La Canada, look for Historic Landmark number 717 in the Clear Creek Vista turnout; a half-mile farther is Clear Creek Junction, where Angeles Forest Highway turns left toward the Mojave Desert.

At 3,300 feet you'll pass Lady Bug Turn, where the road widens and motorists stop in winter to put chains on their tires, required for snow travel. At 13.5 miles is Red Box Saddle, named for the toolbox belonging to firefighters, and the four-mile turnoff to Mount Wilson and the Mount Wilson Observatory telescope, installed between 1904 and 1917 and still in use. Near the telescope are a picnic area and park, and a forest of antennae owned by local television stations rears up from the mountain's highest point.

From the turnoff the road climbs to the crest and at mile twenty-four passes Charlton Flat, a pine-shaded picnic area developed in the 1920s. Chilao Flat campground is two miles farther, and beyond it is the Chilao Visitors Center (open in summer only), with history and nature exhibits, and books and maps for sale. Another mile and you're at Newcomb Ranch, a rambling lodge on private land homesteaded in the last century, where you may be able to get a drink and a sandwich.

The road continues through thick forest for five more miles

to Cloudburst Summit at 7,018 feet, a popular spot for sledding and cross-country skiing, and another mile to Mount Waterman Ski Area, Buckhorn Campground, and Kratka Ski Area. From here the road emerges from the trees along windswept upper slopes and climbs across narrow saddles, with panoramic views to the north and south.

If you want to hike, look for Islip Saddle (about mile forty) and the 2.5-mile trail up 8,214-foot Mount Williamson. From the summit you can look down on the Devil's Punchbowl and the San Andreas Fault snaking along on the edge of the Mojave Desert.

Five and one-half miles farther, at 7,901-foot Dawson Saddle, the road's highest point, you'll pass the trailhead for Throup Peak (pronounced *troop*), named for Amos Throup, the founder of Cal Tech (California Institute of Technology).

Our favorite hike, to the summit of 9,399-foot Mount Baden-Powell, begins at Vincent Gap (mile fifty-three). The 3.5-mile trail switchbacks up through Jeffrey pines and, as you approach the timberline, through a forest of rare 4,000-year-old limber pines. The summit is marked by a stone memorial to Lord Baden-Powell, founder of the Boy Scouts.

Back on the road, take your last scenic photos from Vincent Gap, continue to the ranger station at Big Pines, pass the turnoff for Ski Sunrise on the north side and Mountain High Ski Resort on the south side—they're not open in summer—and end your drive in Wrightwood, a good place for lunch or dinner.

Because we enjoy the Mojave Desert's spare beauty, we drive back to town (Los Angeles) on State 138, which runs north of the mountains and connects to State 14, the Antelope Valley Freeway. You can also cross over Cajon Pass and return on I-10, south of the mountains. The distance is about the same.

Where: In Angeles National Forest.
Hours: No time limit, except during snow season (January

through March), when the center section of the road isn't plowed.
Admission: No charge.
Best time to visit: May through December.
Activities: Scenic viewpoints, picnicking, photography, bird-watching, exhibits and books at the Chilao Visitors Center. Angeles National Forest Maps and Los Angeles County road maps are helpful for getting a sense of location and direction. Topographical maps are recommended for hiking. Maps are sold at the Chilao Visitors Center.
Concessions: Snacks and bathrooms are available at Newcomb Ranch, east of Charlton Flat Picnic Area. The ski resorts are on the south side of the road. Ranger stations are located outside La Canada, Chilao, and Big Pines.
Pets: Allowed on leashes.
For more information:
   Angeles National Forest, 701 North Santa Anita Avenue, Arcadia, CA 91006; 818-574-5200.

San Gabriel Wilderness

Only a few hardy hikers and backpackers are ever privileged enough to experience the remote and rugged interior of the San Gabriel Wilderness, because this 36,118-acre preserve west of State 39 has no roads and few trails. Those who are up to the challenge of bushwhacking, however, find a sometimes impenetrable but unspoiled wilderness of steep canyons, thick pine forests, Douglas fir, alder, and oak, and moist streambeds.
   The region's habitat is a refuge for a variety of animals, particularly black bears, the population of which is estimated at about 300. The original bear population was hunted to extinction years ago, but black bears from the Sierras were reintroduced and have thrived in the rugged backcountry.

The last time we saw a bear—a big male with a thick, red-brown coat—we were camping at Crystal Lake, at the north end of State 39, on the eastern edge of the wilderness.

The bear sprawled across two huge limbs thirty feet up a huge pine, as he lazily watched the half-dozen people standing below and looking up. These black bears aren't tame, but they know they're protected and that people and campgrounds usually mean food. For that reason, the rules for food handling are the same here as elsewhere. Fortunately, encounters between people and bears have been few.

If you do plan to hike in the San Gabriel Wilderness, your choices are limited to a few trails, none of which penetrates the heart of the region. The Devil's Canyon Trail, which begins on the mountain crest at Chilao Flat, twenty-seven miles from La Canada off State 2, drops into a steep canyon for 3.5 miles, following a creek to a trail camp. To return you climb out on the same trail.

From Azusa, you can hike up into the wilderness on the Lower Bear Creek Trail from a point eleven miles north of Azusa; or hike on the Upper Bear Creek Trail, a one-way 11-mile hike that starts 17.5 miles from Azusa, a quarter-mile south of Coldbrook Campground. This strenuous one-way trip, which requires a pickup at the other end, climbs over ridges, follows creekbeds, and descends into canyons, eventually leaving the wilderness at State 39. If you decide to backpack, you can camp anywhere in the forest, as long as you're away from streams and cabins.

Where: Eastern half of Angeles National Forest, north of Arcadia and San Gabriel.
Hours: No limit.
Admission: No fees, except for camping in developed campgrounds.
Best time to visit: Spring and summer.
Activities: Hiking, backpacking, animal identification, bird-

watching, fishing. Mountain biking not allowed in wilderness areas. Wilderness permits aren't required to hike, but are required for camping, backpacking stoves, and grills. Open fires aren't permitted.

Concessions: None.

Pets: Not allowed.

For more information:

Arroyo Seco District, Oak Grove Park, Flintridge, CA 91011; 818-790-1151.

Mount Baldy District, 110 North Wabash, Glendora, CA 91741; 818-335-1251.

Sheep Wilderness

Bring your binoculars when you visit the Sheep Wilderness, 44,000 acres of woodlands and canyons on the south slope of the San Gabriel Mountains, east of and next to the San Gabriel Wilderness. Nelson bighorn sheep are spotted occasionally, but they keep their distance, perching on distant ridges and rocky outcrops.

The highest peak in the San Gabriels, 10,064-foot Mount Baldy (Mount San Antonio), is also in this wilderness, accessible from a trailhead beginning at Mount Baldy Village. The trail up Mount Baldy, one of the most heavily traveled in the forest, is hot, dry, and long, about eleven miles round-trip. It's also very narrow in places, crossing knife-edged ridges above precipitous drops into deep canyons. On the Devil's Backbone, a particularly difficult spot, a metal railing was installed years ago to prevent hikers from falling. The view from the summit is glorious.

To hike into the wilderness from the south, drive to the East Fork Ranger Station north of Glendora, where a number of trails begin. Hikers who know this part of the forest recommend it as both beautiful and remote.

Permits are required for both hiking and camping (except

up Mount Baldy), but you can camp anywhere. Don't hike any-where in these forests without a good trail map or United States Geological Survey topographical map.

Crystal Lake Recreation Area, one of the two busiest desti-nations in the forest, lies between the two wilderness areas at the end of State 39, north of Azusa. A ranger station and visitors center, a campground, and a store are clustered near Crystal Lake. In summer, nature walks and interpretive programs are scheduled. A network of hiking trails fans out from the area, connecting to the Pacific Crest Trail.

Where: Eastern end of Angeles National Forest.
Hours: No limit.
Admission: No fees, except in developed campgrounds.
Best time to visit: Spring and summer.
Activities: Hiking, backpacking, animal viewing, bird-watching, fishing. Mountain biking not allowed. Wilderness permits are required to hike or camp, and for backpacking stoves and grills. Open fires aren't permitted.
Concessions: In Mount Baldy Village, at Mount Baldy Ski Area, at some Angeles National Forest district stations.
Pets: Not allowed.
For more information:
Mount Baldy District, 110 North Wabash, Glendora, CA 91741; 818-335-1251.

Ski Areas In the San Gabriel Mountains

Five ski resorts in the San Gabriel Mountains, all day areas, are small and rustic, but if you're a downhill skier and you like the high country, the combination is unbeatable for a day away from the city. You can be bumper-to-bumper in the middle of down-town Los Angeles at 7:00 A.M. and an hour later standing at the top of Mount Waterman's upper lift amid snow-capped peaks and piney forests.

Three of the resorts have limited snowmaking, two have none; hence they don't open until the first big storms hit Southern California, usually in January. On north-facing slopes, the snow usually remains through April. Four resorts are on the north slope of the San Gabriel Mountains, while the fifth, Mount Baldy, is on the south slope.

Mount Waterman, thirty-four miles east of La Canada on State 2: Our favorite ski area is Mount Waterman, owned by Lynn Newcomb, whose great-great-uncle homesteaded a mountain ranch on the crest of these mountains. A small sign and a parking area mark the bottom of ski lift number one up the face, a steep, mile-long slope with three double–black diamond (expert) runs: two groomed, and one a nightmare of humongous moguls.

But the heart of the resort isn't at the parking lot, but at the top of chair number one, high above in a level meadow, where the lodge and cafeteria, an outdoor picnic area, and a ski-rental hut cluster under the pines. Here, far from the road, where the only sounds are the wind in the pines and skis swishing on snow, you're in a whole different world.

Two other lifts leading to intermediate runs start here, dropping into canyons toward the side and along the upper slopes of the mountain. A snack bar in the lodge serves hamburgers and chili.

Kratka Ridge, thirty-six miles east of La Canada on State 2: Kratka Ridge is two miles east of Waterman on an equally steep slope. Though the resort is tiny, it's a popular practice location for local ski racers. The owners of both Waterman and Kratka would like to expand their facilities, but would have to renegotiate their Forest Service leases. Kratka has one double chair, one single, and a rope tow. The longest run is a half mile. Food is available.

Ski Sunrise, six miles west of Wrightwood on State 2: Ski Sunrise is a family affair, with mostly intermediate and beginner slopes, snowmaking, one quad lift and two surface lifts, a restaurant, and ski rentals. The longest run is one mile. There's more variety here, but the resort is crowded on weekends.

Mountain High, three miles west of Wrightwood on State 2: This is the biggest resort in the San Gabriels and the closest to the town of Wrightwood, where skiers rent cabins for winter holidays. The resort, the busiest and most commercial, has a restaurant, rentals, snowmaking, mostly intermediate runs, a high-speed quad lift, a quad chair, three triple chairs, and six double chairs. The longest run is 1.5 miles.

Mount Baldy Ski Area, on the south slope of the San Gabriels, 16 miles north of Upland on Mountain Avenue: Mount Baldy has lots of varied terrain and some sensationally steep slopes famous for extreme skiing, but only after a snowstorm has dumped on the mountain. Snowmaking covers some slopes, but Mount Baldy, on a south slope, is often at the mercy of Mother Nature. Baldy has ski rentals, two restaurants, and four double chairlifts. The longest run is 2.5 miles.

Where: All resorts are in the San Gabriel Mountains.
Hours: Day skiing only. No night skiing.
Admission: $25 to $32 for lift tickets.
Best time to visit: January through April.
Activities: Skiing, lessons, snowboarding.
Concessions: Ski school, restaurants, warming lodge, equipment rentals. Waterman and Kratka are day areas only. The other three are near cabin and condominium rentals.
Pets: Not allowed off leashes.
For more information:
   Mount Waterman, 818-790-2002.
   Kratka Ridge, 818-449-1749.
   Ski Sunrise, 619-249-6150.

Mountain High, 619-249-5477.
Mount Baldy, 909-981-3344.

CASTAIC LAKE STATE RECREATION AREA

Castaic Lake, a huge man-made reservoir with twenty-nine miles of shoreline and an estimated 323,702 acre-feet of water, reaches into two rugged canyons in the dry foothills near the western end of the San Gabriel Mountains.

Castaic stores drinking water for parched Southern California, but it serves two other purposes, as well. The reservoir, a popular water-sports area, is a fishing lake where for the last decade local anglers have been catching record-setting bass, the largest in the country.

The east arm of the main reservoir, 320 feet at the deepest point, is reserved for sailboats and fishing boats. The west arm is reserved for speedboats and waterskiing.

Below the dam, a smaller lake, the "lagoon," is designated for shore fishing, small-boat sailing, windsurfing, electric-powered boats, and jet skis; a grassy area beside the parking lot has picnic tables. A swimming beach here used to be jammed with local residents on 108-degree summer days, but persistent problems with bacterial growth prompted authorities to close it down.

The lake's first fish arrived on their own, swimming south along the canal and through the pumps from the Sacramento River Delta, but the California Department of Fish and Game now stocks it with other warm-water species: bass, crappie, and catfish. You can bring your own boat or rent one at the East Launch ramp, open every day year-round. In summer, the West Launch ramp opens on weekends for overflow traffic.

If you were here in the early 1980s, you may remember stopping at the visitors center on a peak above the lake. Recently the center was closed, and some of the exhibits were moved to the new visitors center at Pyramid Lake.

Where: On State 126, forty-one miles from downtown Los Angeles on I-5.
Hours: Daily, year-round.
Admission: $6 per vehicle.
Best time to visit: Year-round.
Activities: Fishing and water sports. No swimming.
Concessions: Boat rentals, supplies, and food available at the East Launch ramp.
Pets: Allowed on leashes.
For more information:

Castaic Lake State Recreation Area, 805-257-4050.

East Launch ramp concessionaire, 805-257-2049.

Saugus District, Angeles National Forest, 30800 Bouquet Canyon Road, Saugus, CA 91350; 805-296-9710.

PYRAMID LAKE RECREATION AREA

One of Southern California's most compelling tales is the story of the ambitious engineering scheme that brought water from Northern California over the mountains to the semiarid valleys of Southern California, making the growth of a vast metropolitan area possible.

At the Vista Del Lago Visitors Center at Pyramid Lake, one of the project's larger reservoirs, elevation 2,578 feet, you can learn the story of the California State Water Project from photos and exhibits—then spend the rest of the day swimming, fishing, sailing, or waterskiing.

The 18,500-square-foot visitors center, on a ridge above the reservoir, houses offices and exhibits, with maps, photos, diagrams, and an eighteen-minute color film detailing the project's network of canals, pumping stations, dams, and power plants.

The source of the lake is water that flows 400 miles south from the Sacramento and San Joaquin River Deltas. At the south end of the San Joaquin Valley, huge pumps lift it over the Tehachapi Mountains and into two channels, diverting the west branch to Pyramid and Castaic Lakes and the east branch to Silverwood Lake and Lake Perris.

Unfortunately, Pyramid Lake, formed by a dam across Piru Creek, covers the most spectacular portion of the canyon through which Old Highway 99 between Los Angeles and Bakersfield used to run. The highway was replaced by Interstate 5, the only north-south road in the area. After the Northridge Earthquake in January 1994, many traffic experts wished that Old 99 had been kept open for emergencies.

To stop at the visitors center, leave I-5 at the Vista Del Lago exit, sixteen miles north of Castaic, and cross to the west side of the freeway. You can't miss the hexagonal, adobe-colored structure and red tile roof. To go down to the lake, return to I-5, exit at Hungry Valley/Smokey Bear west, and follow the road down to the lake. "Hungry Valley," the road's historic name dating from 1852, has been renamed "Smokey Bear" to commemorate the fiftieth birthday of the black bear that became the symbol of America's great outdoors, but spent his life in a zoo.

Although Pyramid has 1,300 acres of surface area, only fifty boats are allowed on the water at any one time. Why? The parking lot holds only fifty cars. Why not enlarge it? "Budget cuts," says a Forest Service employee in the modern new visitors center.

Pyramid is a multiuse lake, for sailboats, speedboats with waterskiers, motorboats, and anglers. Jet skiing is allowed, but canoes aren't. You can swim in designated areas when lifeguards are on duty.

Where: Fifty miles north of Los Angeles on the west side of I-5, off Hungry Valley Road.
Hours: Dawn to dusk.

Admission: Daytime use is $4 per car. Camping and boating fees are separate.

Best time to visit: Summer is very hot. Winter is pleasant.

Activities: Boating, waterskiing, jet skiing, fishing, picnicking, camping.

Concessions: The marina and Los Alamos Campground are operated by a concessionaire. Campgrounds in Angeles National Forest are managed by the Forest Service. Boat ramps, rest rooms, and picnic areas are provided at several sites.

Pets: Allowed on leashes.

For more information:

Vista Del Lago Visitors Center, 805-294-0219.

Marina and Los Alamos Campground, 805-257-2892.

Saugus District, Angeles National Forest, 30800 Bouquet Canyon Road, Saugus, CA 91350; 805-296-9710.

FORT TEJON STATE HISTORIC PARK

Fort Tejon, a historic military fort in a grove of 500-year-old oaks at the head of Grapevine Canyon, once guarded Tejon Pass and the principal route from Southern California north to Sacramento.

Today the 205-acre historic park and its restored military buildings are a reminder of the days of wagon and horseback travel, when controlling roads and mountain passes was the first rule of military strategy.

The fort stands at the intersection of two major earthquake faults, the San Andreas and the Garlock. On January 9, 1857, an enormous earthquake occurred here at 6:30 A.M., destroying the officers' quarters and damaging the hospital, the storehouse, and other buildings. The tremors lasted for three minutes, and in some places the San Andreas Fault slipped thirty feet.

In a letter to *The Los Angeles Star*, Quartermaster's Deputy

Alonzo Wakeman wrote that "immense trees have been snapped off . . . and every building between Fort Tejon and Lake Elizabeth [is] leveled with the ground. . . . Many persons have been seriously injured, and one woman killed at Reed's Rancho."

Tejon Pass had been discovered eighty-five years earlier, in 1772, by members of the Pedro Fages expedition, who recorded the event in a trip log. In 1852, the R. S. Williamson Survey mapped the mountains for a railroad route (never built), and the fort was constructed two years later. During the Civil War, when many Californians supported the Confederate cause, Union soldiers were stationed at Fort Tejon.

At the war's end, the military abandoned the fort, but the road through the mountains continued to be a main north-south route for wagons and stagecoaches. The road was eventually paved, renamed US 99 in 1933, and later widened as Interstate 5.

To visit the fort, on I-5 north of Frazier Park, turn west at the Fort Tejon exit and follow signs to the parking lot, a brass State Historic Marker commemorating the site and the entrance. The park is beyond in a protected valley, with picnic areas and restored adobe barracks, stables, a munitions storehouse, a jailhouse, and officers' quarters.

On the first Sunday of the month between April and October, docents in period costume recreate frontier life. On the third Sunday, the fort is the site of authentic reenactments of Civil War battles and encampments, with participants attired in historic dress and armed with period weapons. Visitors are invited to watch the mock battles and tour the camp area.

Where: Seventy-six miles northwest of Los Angeles, north of Frazier Park, on the west side of I-5 at the Fort Tejon exit.
Hours: 10:00 A.M. to 4:00 P.M.
Admission: $2 per person.
Best time to visit: April through October.
Activities: Tours of the buildings, picnicking.

Concessions: Gift shop and museum exhibits. No food is available, but picnicking on the grass is allowed.
Pets: Allowed on leashes; not allowed in buildings.
For more information:
   Fort Tejon State Historic Park, P.O. Box 895, Lebec CA 93243; 805-248-6692.

SAN BERNARDINO NATIONAL FOREST

San Bernardino National Forest, divided into two sections over four mountain ranges, covers a huge area, with 810,287 acres of land within boundaries and 633,423 dedicated forest acres.

   The northern half, fifty miles long from east to west, ranges from the end of the San Gabriel Mountains east across the great arc of the San Bernardino Mountains. Elevations soar from 1,300 feet in the foothills to 11,499 feet at the top of Mount San Gorgonio, Southern California's highest peak. The range separates San Bernardino Valley on the south from the Mojave Desert on the north.

   The southern half of the forest, in Riverside County south of I-5, also encompasses two ranges. The first is the San Jacinto Mountains, a north-south range and the northernmost of the peninsular ranges that continue south into San Diego County. The San Jacintos' high country is divided between national-forest wilderness and state-park wilderness.

   The second range is the Santa Rosa Mountains, which rise steeply from sea level west of the Salton Sea to 8,046 feet at the summit. The Santa Rosas cross into San Diego County and the northeast corner of Anza-Borrego Desert State Park, where they're designated a state wilderness.

   The Land: A tremendous variety of terrain and elevation makes this national forest and its mountains the region's boldest and most beautiful, with vegetation ranging from semiarid desert plants to alpine flowers.

At low elevations are Joshua trees and barrel cactus, pinyon pine, juniper, and sagebrush; higher up are lowland-oak meadows and chaparral foothills. On the highest slopes are white pine and fir, with a stand of ancient limber pines on the upper slopes of the San Gorgonio Wilderness. A half-dozen natural lakes are tucked into deep canyons, helping to feed year-round streams. On the rocky peaks, small patches of snow last until late summer.

Recreation: An estimated six million visitors use San Bernardino National Forest each year, hiking, mountain biking, fishing, boating, skiing in winter, camping in one of twenty-four developed campgrounds, and vacationing in rental cabins or at resorts.

The busiest and largest recreation area is around Big Bear Lake, a large lake in a valley along the top of a ridge, surrounded on three sides by private land with towns, homes, rental cabins, ski areas, resorts, and marinas.

The largest outdoor recreation area is at Barton Flats, the jumping-off point for the San Gorgonio Wilderness, where you'll find campgrounds and trailheads. A third, smaller recreation area is located near Lake Arrowhead, west of Big Bear Lake, and in Idyllwild, in the southern half of the forest.

Hiking: There are 570 miles of trails in San Bernardino National Forest, many concentrated in two areas, the San Gorgonio Wilderness and the Big Bear Lake vicinity. The Pacific Crest Trail runs for 146 miles across the forest, entering it on the western border, traveling north of Big Bear Lake, then turning south at Nelson Ridge to cross I-10 toward the San Jacinto Mountains.

Permits are free, but required if you want to hike in wilderness areas. In 1971, forest rangers instituted the wilderness permit system to control the number of people using backcountry trails.

Bird-watching is also popular; a partial list of species includes bald and golden eagles, red-tailed and red-shouldered hawks, turkey vultures, owls, grebes, coots, kestrels, killdeer, poorwills, flickers, woodpeckers (acorn, downy, hairy, ladder-backed, and white-headed), phoebes, woodthrashers, jays, gnat-catchers, and hummingbirds.

Grizzly bears by the hundreds once roamed the San Bernardinos, their numbers limited only by food supplies. Now the list of animals has been reduced to sixty-one species, including the California ground squirrel, western gray squirrel, deer mouse, skunk, black bear, coyote, mule deer, Nelson bighorn sheep, and bobcat, plus varieties of mice, rabbits, and bats. Badgers, ringtailed foxes, kit foxes, beavers, and mountain lions are seen more rarely.

Like raccoons, ringtails will eat almost anything from lizards to fruit

History: The first explorers crossed the mountains in 1845; by 1860, when gold was discovered in Holcomb Valley, settlers were beginning to arrive. By 1893, when the first forest reserve was created, hunting, fishing, and timbering had depleted natural resources. In 1908, San Bernardino National Forest was created.

As early as 1931, the San Gorgonio high country was awarded a special "wild" status. More recently, the area was enlarged and added to the national wilderness system. Three other wildernesses are within the forest, as well: the Cucamonga, the Santa Rosa, and the San Jacinto.

Where: In San Bernardino and Riverside Counties.

Hours: No limit.

Admission: No fee to enter or hike. Fees for camping.

Best time to visit: Year-round. The high country is often closed by snow in winter.

Activities: Hiking, backpacking, mountain biking, camping, skiing, bird-watching, animal identification, picnicking. Permits are required for day and overnight hiking in wilderness areas. Cooking fires are allowed only with a permit. Backpacking stoves are recommended.

Concessions: Located around private recreation areas, primarily near Big Bear Lake and Idyllwild.

Pets: Allowed on leashes; not allowed on trails in wilderness areas.

For more information:

San Bernardino Forest Supervisor, 144 North Mountain View Avenue, San Bernardino, CA 92408; 909-393-5588.

Arrowhead District, P.O. Box 7, Rim Forest, CA 92378; 909-337-2444.

Big Bear District, P.O. Box 290, Fawnskin, CA 92333; 909-866-3437.

Cajon District, Star Route Box 100, Fontana, CA 92335; 909-887-2576.

San Gorgonio District, Route 1 Box 264, Mentone, CA 92359; 909-794-1123.

San Jacinto District, P.O. Box 518, Idyllwild, CA 92349; 909-659-2117.

Cucamonga Wilderness Area: This small wilderness area, straddling the Angeles–San Bernardino National Forest border, is made up of 4,400 acres in the former and 8,581 acres in the latter. The most-used trails begin at Icehouse Canyon in Angeles National Forest; the trail to the summits of the "Three Ts" – Timber, Telegraph, and Thunder Peaks – is one of them.

The Big Tree trailhead, on the southern border, starts at Joe Elliott Camp off Forest Road 1N34. On the eastern boundary, the Middle Fork Trail starts at the end of Middle Fork Lytle Creek (Road 2N58), out of Apple White Picnic Area.

San Gorgonio Wilderness Area: The San Gorgonio Wilderness, 58,969 acres in size, unmarred by roads or tourist concessions, encircles Mount San Gorgonio and the high country above 9,500 feet. With a range of terrain varying from tall forests cut by rushing creeks to sculpted basins above the timberline, a variety of hiking trails make this wilderness the most heavily trafficked area of San Bernardino National Forest.

Approximately 100 miles of trails begin near Jenks Lake at Barton Flats, on State 38. Fanning out, they climb into the high country past lakes and over meadows to the mountain summits. In winter, the level meadows around Barton Flats are favored by cross-country skiers.

The busiest trail is the South Fork Trail to the summit of 11,499-foot Mount San Gorgonio, a twenty-one-mile hike that most people make in two days, camping out halfway up.

To make the climb, exit I-10 at State 38, drive north, stop at the Mill Creek Ranger Station just past Mentone for a wilderness permit and a hiking map, continue ten miles to Jenks Lake Road, and turn right. The South Fork trailhead is three miles farther on. If you don't want to climb to the summit, day hikes to Dollar Lake and Dry Lake cross through some of the prettiest country.

Four Forest Service campgrounds at Barton Flats have tent and RV sites up to sixteen and thirty feet, with toilets, piped water, tables, and fire rings.

Where: In the north section of San Bernardino Forest, southeast corner directly north of Banning.
Hours: No limit.
Admission: No fee to hike.
Best time to visit: Year-round.
Activities: Hiking, backpacking, cross-country skiing, animal identification. Camping allowed in designated areas only.
Concessions: None in the wilderness areas.
Pets: Not allowed.
For more information:
  San Gorgonio District, Route 1, Box 264, Mentone, CA 92359; 909-794-1123.

Santa Rosa Wilderness Area: This semiarid roadless region, 19,803 acres in the far southeast corner of San Bernardino National Forest, belongs more to the desert than to the mountains, and more to the desert bighorn sheep, for which this is a safe haven, than to man.

In elevations from 3,200 feet to 7,600 feet, Colorado Desert vegetation flourishes on the lower slopes, chaparral at middle elevations, and pine forests on the upper slopes. Flash floods are common after thunderstorms, summer is blisteringly hot, and in winter snow falls occasionally at upper elevations.

The area's single hiking trail, the Cactus Spring Trail, is a rough path that runs across the wilderness from the northwest to the southeast corner. A traditional Native American trail, it was used by early Cahuilla people, whose descendants still live on the Santa Rosa Reservation just west of the wilderness area.

The trail gets occasional maintenance, and, although it disappears in places, it's identified by wood markers and rock cairns. If you hike this way, use a topographical map (available from national-forest ranger offices) and a compass, wear a hat and protective clothing, and carry a gallon of water per person per day.

To hike from the west end, take State 74 to Forest Road 7S09, south of the Pinyon Flat Campground turnoff. Go to the first fork, turn left onto a dirt road, and park between the Pinyon Flats Waste Disposal Station and Elk's Retreat. To hike from the east end, park next to the Sugarloaf Cafe on State 74 and look for the trail.

Where: Southeast corner of San Bernardino National Forest, in Riverside County, east of Alpine Village and south of Palm Desert.
Hours: No limit.
Admission: No fee.
Best time to visit: Spring and fall.
Activities: Hiking, desert exploration.
Concessions: None. Pinyon Flats Campground is the closest improved campground, to the west off State 74.
Pets: Not permitted in wilderness areas.
For more information:
San Jacinto Ranger District, P.O. Box 518, 54270 Pinecrest, Idyllwild, CA 92549; 909-659-2117.

San Jacinto Wilderness State Park and National Forest Wilderness Area: It was a clear, hot morning in July when we hiked past the granite dome of Tahquitz Rock (also called Lily Rock), in the San Jacinto Mountains, heading for the Pacific Crest Trail and the summit of 10,804-foot Mount San Jacinto.

As we climbed up a steep switchback, the wind rustled the pine trees, grasshoppers buzzed in the brush, and the steady tap of a woodpecker drilling for insects echoed across the meadow. But not another human being was to be seen.

The hike to the summit of "San Jack" from the trailhead at Humber Park is probably the most widely known trek along the 275 miles of trails that wind through these mountains. The trails lie protected within four adjacent parks: San Bernardino National Forest, San Jacinto Wilderness Area, Mount San Jacinto State Wilderness Park, and a county park. Hiking and permit regulations vary slightly from one park to another, but you're not conscious of borders as you hike among these lofty peaks, across alpine meadows, and through green woods.

In the center of the forest on private land is Idyllwild, population 2,500, with three main streets and a collection of cabins and stores. Despite its rustic charm, the town has never become a fast-track tourist destination, evolving instead into an art community with galleries, shops, and quaint bed and breakfasts.

Beyond the village is the wilderness, where hiking, backpacking, mountain biking, and rock climbing are the only summer activities and cross-country skiing the main winter sport. Lake Hemet is farther south on State 74, which crosses the national forest from northwest to southeast. The lake, two miles long, is a fishing destination with bass, catfish, and trout. Only small boats are permitted, and there's no swimming. A campground and a supply store are on the north shore.

The mountains: The northernmost of the peninsular ranges, the San Jacinto Mountains' northeast slope rears up like a wall from an elevation of 2,000 feet on the desert floor to above 10,000 feet, the steepest escarpment in North America. With such tremendous elevation changes and six separate vegetation zones, this range is a botanist's dream.

At the base of the mountains is the Colorado Desert, with creosote bushes and ironwood trees; next the Upper Sonoran zone, with chamise, manzanita, and scrub oak; then a transition zone of ponderosa, Jeffrey, Coulter, and sugar pines and California black oak. Above that are two narrow vegetation belts, the Canadian and Hudsonian zones, with mixed lodgepole and limber pine. Finally, on the summit of Mount San Jacinto is a small arctic-alpine zone, with alpine ground cover and dwarf flowers.

Day trips: To tour the mountains by car on a day trip, drive up from I-5 on State 243 and leave on State 74 (or the reverse), stopping in Idyllwild for lunch. If time permits, stay overnight in town or camp out, and include at least one day hike.

Don't pass up the County Park Nature Center, a half mile north of Idyllwild on State 243, where geological exhibits, stuffed birds, and Native American artifacts occupy well-lighted and attractive display cases. The rangers show a nature film hourly ($1 admission) and post a schedule of daytime nature walks and evening programs, held under the stars in the amphitheater below the campground.

Hiking and camping: A one-mile self-guided hike along the Yellow Pine Forest Nature Trail begins here at the Nature Center. Several longer hikes begin at Humber Park, on the edge of town. If the lot is full you can park along the road.

Hikers need a free permit from the ranger station before going onto the trails; the purpose is to limit use. Backpackers also need a permit and can camp only in designated campsites. Mountain bikers can use forty miles of trails and 200 miles of dirt roads outside the wilderness areas.

There are two campgrounds in town: the county-park campground on the south side (ninety sites) and the state-park campground on the north side (thirty sites). Other campgrounds are scattered around the national forest.

Palm Springs Aerial Tramway: If you don't mind heights, an amazing and memorable way to see the face of the mountains is a ride on the Palm Springs Aerial Tramway, a cable car that ascends from the desert floor at 2,643 feet to Long Valley at 8,516 feet, flying 13,800 feet up the nearly vertical front slope in fourteen minutes flat.

Board at Valley Station in Chino Canyon, six miles from Palm Springs off State 111; you exit at the mountain station amid pine forests and cool breezes. Many hikers climb San Jacinto from this side, saving themselves the long grind up the back.

Where: Off State 243, south of I-5 near Banning, or north of State 74 near Hemet.

Hours: Ranger stations and campground kiosks are open during business hours. The Palm Springs Aerial Tramway runs from 10:00 A.M. to 9:00 P.M. on weekdays and 8:00 A.M. to 9:00 P.M. on weekends.

Admission: No charge for hiking and camping permits. National-forest and state-campground fees vary. Tramway rides (round-trip) are $10 to $15.

Best time to visit: Spring, summer, fall.

Activities: Hiking, backpacking, mountain biking, rock climbing. Free permits are required for all hiking and backpacking. Bicycles are restricted to forty miles of trails and 200 miles of dirt roads.

Concessions: The town of Idyllwild has inns, bed and breakfasts, restaurants, markets, bike-rental shops, an outdoor-sports store, and a rock-climbing center. Horseback riding can be arranged. Forest Service campgrounds are first-come first-served. Reservations suggested for state-park campgrounds.

Pets: Allowed in most areas.

For more information:

Idyllwild Chamber of Commerce, P.O. Box 3396, Idyllwild, CA 92549; 909-659-8525 or 659-3259.

U.S. Forest Service, P.O. Box 518, Idyllwild, CA 92349; 909-659-2117.

Mount San Jacinto State Wilderness Park, P.O. Box 308, Idyllwild, CA 92349; 909-659-2607.

BIG BEAR LAKE AREA

While the August heat melts the asphalt on Ventura Boulevard in Los Angeles, cool breezes waft over seven-mile-long Big Bear Lake, at 6,754 feet in the northern half of San Bernardino National Forest. In the distance, waterskiers skim the surface; on the far shore, golfers on Bear Mountain's nine-hole public course putt amid the rustle of pine needles.

Recreation is the name of the game at this man-made mountain lake, one of Southern California's prime vacation destinations, a couple of hours' drive from the city center. Tourism, in fact, is the valley's lifeblood, supported by more than 100 motels, cottages, lodges, and resorts located on private land along the south and east shores.

Whether you're camping in a national-forest campground on the north shore or in a resort on the south shore, start with a two-hour lake cruise on board the paddle wheeler *Big Bear Queen*, with Captain Dave Bellows at the helm.

For the price of a ticket, Bellows relates the valley's history, points out the lakeside mansions of film stars, explores every bay, and shows you 11,499 foot, snow-capped San Gorgonio in the distance. He also tells you where to waterski, windsurf, parasail, camp, and swim, and reminds you that to fish for trout and bass you need a California state fishing license.

The official Big Bear story is also the theme at the Big Bear Museum's exhibits on ranching, gold mining, and Native American culture. The museum, in Big Bear City Park, is open Saturdays from 10:00 A.M. to 4:00 P.M. and Sundays and holidays from 1:00 to 4:00 P.M. Admission is free.

The valley, on top of the long level crest of the northern San Bernardino Mountains, was a wilderness until 1845, when Benamin Wilson, a rancher, and a posse of twenty-two Mexican cavalry (California was part of Mexico then) rode through the area in search of cattle rustlers. When the bandits vanished, the posse decided to go hunting, bagging twenty-two grizzly bears (one per man) before heading home.

Later, lumbermen logged the timber, and, in 1860, a gold strike in Holcomb Valley, north of the lake, sparked a gold rush. Finally, in 1884, the city of Redlands built the first dam at the valley's west end, creating the present lake as a source of water for the orange groves below and sprouting a new industry — tourism.

The lake's north shore, where San Bernardino National Forest comes down to the water, is relatively undeveloped, with campgrounds, trailheads, a paved bikepath, public swimming beaches, marinas, and docks. The road to Holcomb Valley also begins here.

For a self-guided driving tour of the miners' shacks and mine sites, pick up a copy of the Gold Fever Trail map at the ranger station on State 38. If you plan to walk, get a free hiking-trail map at the same place. To let a horse do the work for you, Baldwin Lake Stables and Big Bear Riding Stable, both in Big Bear City at the lake's east end, offer guided one- and two-hour trail rides. But lately, the hottest sport in town is mountain biking at Snow Summit Ski Resort.

The ski resort's two longest lifts ferry bikes and riders (and hikers and sightseers) to the summit and the start of sixty miles of tough and tame trails and dirt roads. Business is so brisk that the ski resort keeps the View Haus Café, at the peak, open all summer. One of life's great pleasures is eating lunch on the deck in midsummer, amid panoramic views of the rumpled crest of the mountains.

Where: On State 38, northeast of San Bernardino.
Best time to visit: Spring for wildflowers; summer for water sports; fall for the foliage; winter for skiing.
Activities: Camping, hiking, water sports, horseback riding, skiing, shopping.

Concessions: Restaurants, hotels, cottages, markets, and supply stores are along the south shore. For accommodations call 909-866-7000. For lake cruises on the *Big Bear Queen*: tickets are $8.50 for adults, $6.50 for children; call 909-866-3218. For waterskiing and parasailing at Knight's Pine Knot Water Ski School: $45 per half-hour; call 909-585-7580.

For mountain biking at Snow Summit Ski Resort: one-way tickets are $7 with bike, $4.50 without; seniors $3 and $2. Round-trip ticket, no bike, $7. All-day pass with bike, $16. Bike rental (includes helmet) from Team Big Bear, $6.50 per hour, $22 half day, $32 full day. Driver's license and credit card required; call 909-866-4565.

To play golf at Bear Mountain Golf Course on Moonridge Road: greens fees are $12-$16; call 909-585-8002. For horseback riding at Big Bear Riding Stable: trail rides are $12 per hour; call 909-585-1260. At Baldwin Lake Stables: $15 per hour; call 909-585-6482.

Pets: Allowed in the town of Big Bear Lake, allowed on leashes in the National Forest; not allowed in wilderness areas.

For more information:

Big Bear Lake Chamber of Commerce, P.O. Box 2860, Big Bear Lake, CA 92315; 909-866-7000.

San Bernardino National Forest Ranger Station (on State 38), 909-866-3437.

LAKE ARROWHEAD

While Lake Arrowhead, shimmering in the summer sun at 4,114 feet elevation, invites you to stop and tarry awhile, there's limited public recreation available here. Private vacation properties occupy most of the lakeshore, and public resort facilities have been discouraged. You can occasionally find rental cabins or houses for summer or winter vacations, however, and there are a couple of resort hotels.

Beavers sharing a meal

Public boat ramps around the lake allow access, and fishing is available. Fifty-minute narrated boat tours of the lake leave hourly in summer from the Lake Arrowhead Village waterfront.

Where: Off State 18 on the north border of San Bernardino National Forest.

Hours: No limit.

Admission: Lake tours are $9.50 for adults, $8.50 for seniors, $6.50 for children ages two to twelve; tickets at LeRoy's Sports in the village.

Best time to visit: Year-round.

Activities: Limited. A nice place for lunch and snapping photos.

Concessions: Limited to local markets and cafés.

Pets: Allowed.

For more information:

LeRoy's Sports, 909-336-6992.

SKI RESORTS IN THE SAN BERNARDINO MOUNTAINS

Don't turn up your nose at skiing in the San Bernardino Mountains until you've tried the two biggest resorts, Snow Summit and Bear Mountain. These two ski areas, on adjacent 8,000-foot mountains, are as big and modern as many small ski resorts elsewhere, and the only drawback to skiing here is that weekends and holidays are unbearably crowded. If at all possible, come during the week.

Both resorts have installed snowmaking equipment on most runs, and both lay down a two-foot base of snow in November, when nighttime temperatures drop into the teens and twenties. The water, which comes from the lake, melts and returns to the lake in spring or drains into the water table. By January, when the first snowstorms arrive, there's enough base to capture and keep natural snow.

Bear Mountain has a high-speed quad lift on the lower, most heavily used run, and both have standard quad, triple, and double chairs on all runs. While some skiers come up for a single day, the town of Big Bear Lake survives in winter by renting hundreds of cabins, condos, and lodges for longer ski vacations.

A third large resort, Snow Valley, is west of Big Bear Lake

near Running Springs. The resort matches its two rivals in size and runs (and also has standard quad, triple, and double lifts), but with a limited supply of water for snowmaking, it must depend on Mother Nature. The resort is currently acquiring other water resources. Snow Valley is a great place to ski – but check the snow levels before going.

Two other tiny, family ski resorts, Snow Forest and Green Valley, are near Big Bear Lake. The clientele at these areas is mostly local residents.

Snow Summit, one mile east of the town of Big Bear Lake, on Summit Boulevard, off State 18: This number-one-rated resort has sixty-five percent intermediate runs and twenty-five percent advanced, with a longest run of 1.25 miles. There are three quad chairs, three triples, and five doubles. Snowmaking is top quality. Rentals, restaurant, lodge.

Bear Mountain, one mile southeast of Big Bear Lake on Moonridge Road off State 18: Bear Mountain's 8805-foot summit is the highest of all the resorts, while its longest run is two miles. One high-speed quad, three triple chairs, and four doubles service runs that are fifty percent intermediate and twenty-five percent expert. Rentals, restaurants, lodge.

Snow Valley, five miles east of Running Springs on State 18: With the number of beginning, intermediate, and expert runs divided equally, Snow Valley has something for every skier. The longest run is 1.25 miles, and there are five triple chairs and eight doubles. This resort, the only one with night skiing, also has snowmaking, rentals, a restaurant, and a lodge.

Where: In the San Bernardino Mountains, near Big Bear Lake.
Hours: Daylight; Snow Valley also has night skiing.
Admission: Adult tickets are $35 per day and up. Frequent discounts offered.
Best time to visit: November through April.

Activities: Skiing, snowboarding, lessons, NASTAR races, celebrity fund-raising events.

Concessions: Equipment rentals, ski school, restaurants, lodge and beer bars, ski shops.

Pets: Not allowed.

For more information:

Snow Summit, 909-866-5766.

Bear Mountain, 909-585-2519.

Snow Valley, 909-867-2751.

SILVERWOOD LAKE STATE RECREATION AREA

Silverwood Lake and Recreation Area, at an elevation of 3,378 feet on the north slope of the San Bernardino Mountains above the Mojave Desert, is the highest reservoir in the California State Water Project.

Shaped like a massive oak tree with a wide base, thick trunk, and large crown, the lake is much bigger than it looks as you stand on the shore near the campgrounds. The reservoir holds 75,000 acre-feet, or 25 billion gallons, of water, which travels 400 miles south from the Sacramento River Delta, in Northern California, to get here.

Silverwood's visitor facilities are on the lakeshore at the base of the "tree"; they include a campground, a marina, two swimming areas, boat rentals and slips, a store, and a snack bar. The "trunk" of the lake is a passageway for boats traveling between the marina and the main lake, the "crown." The open water near the dam is reserved for speedboating and waterskiing, and for fishing near the shoreline.

The lake was formed by Cedar Springs Dam, 249 feet high, which blocks the canyon carved by the north fork of the Mojave River. Though national-forest land surrounds the recreation area, this north side of the mountain range has a semidesert climate, with chaparral on most lower slopes.

In summer the days are very hot, and the nights are temperate. In winter, the days are sunny and mild, while the nights are quite cold. Most rain falls between November and April; the other months are generally dry and sunny.

Because hikers and wilderness campers don't usually like the noise and paraphernalia associated with motorboating, Silverwood is claimed mostly by boat owners and fishermen.

The California Department of Fish and Game stocks the lake with trout, largemouth bass, catfish, and bluegills. The best fishing is by boat; you can rent one from the concessionaire if you want to fish in the far portions of the lake; recent prices included $28 for a full day.

If you come for the day, you can sign up for a guided boat tour around the lake's thirteen-mile perimeter, perhaps the best way to see some of the 130 bird species park rangers have identified. As wetlands have diminished, lakes like Silverwood have become important stopovers and wintering sites for migratory birds, as well as permanent habitats for resident birds. Canada geese and other waterfowl winter here, and bald and golden eagles fish in the lake. Other raptors and songbirds are permanent residents.

Four picnic areas—Black Oak, Manzanita, Chaparral, and Willows—are accessible by car. Three others—Live Oak, Chamise, and Sycamore—can be reached only by boat.

Twelve miles of hiking trails start from the area, but are used primarily by joggers. Families and reunion groups can reserve one of three large group camps in Miller Canyon.

Where: On State 138, eleven miles east of I-15.
Hours: Check-in during daylight hours. Boats are allowed on the lake between 7:00 A.M. and 7:00 P.M.
Admission: $6 entry fee per vehicle. Camp sites are extra.
Best time to visit: May through October.
Activities: Fishing, boating, swimming, sunning, camping.
Concessions: 136 developed campsites. A boat-launch ramp,

A female white-tailed kite

boarding docks, boat slips, boat and equipment rentals, a supply store, a snack bar, and a ranger station are close to the campgrounds.

Pets: Allowed on leashes only.

For more information:

Silverwood Lake State Recreation Area, 619-389-2303 or 619-389-2281.

Marina information, 619-389-2320.

LAKE PERRIS STATE RECREATION AREA

In arid Southern California, where fresh water is scarce and lakes are prized for recreation, 2,000-acre Lake Perris is no exception. The lake, a reservoir in a low valley, is enclosed by grass-covered hills (the Russell Mountains and the Bernasconi Hills), climbing to 1,575 feet at their highest elevation.

Lately we've stopped here for the day to swim, but we used to camp out with a rock-climbing club. Then and now the rock formations south of Perris Dam are in demand with novice climbers playing Spiderman on weekends.

Most visitors to the 8,800-acre recreation area aren't climbers, however, but small-sailboat and motorboat owners, who trailer their boats and make a weekend of camping, fishing, and waterskiing.

Windsurfers have discovered Lake Perris and are out in force, as well. Big lakes like this one that cater to motorboats aren't really wilderness, but when you're out on the water under a blue sky and warm sun, it's a satisfyingly good imitation of the real thing.

Lake Perris, the last reservoir for water storage in the east branch of the chain of reservoirs and dams managed by the California State Water Project, is stocked with rainbow trout, Alabama spotted bass, crappie, catfish, and bluegills, most of which thrive on their own.

Though the reservoirs and lakes in the water project originally had no fish populations, it took just a couple of years for adaptable species, including green sunfish and shrimp, to migrate from one lake to another.

If you want to know something about the original inhabitants of the Mojave Desert region (the Cahuilla, Chemehuevi, Cupeno, Luiseno, Serrano, and Vanyume Native American tribes), stop at the Regional Indian Museum, which contains exhibits and artifacts.

Where: Eleven miles south of Riverside, near State 60 or I-215.

Hours: Check-in time between 8:00 A.M. and 6:00 P.M.

Admission: $6 per car for daytime use. Overnight camping follows California State Park guidelines: $14 per night in the low season, $16 per night from Memorial Day to Labor Day.

Best time to visit: Swimmers and sailboarders like summer. Fishermen and rock climbers prefer winter.

Activities: Hiking, biking, fishing, sailing, sailboarding, water-skiing, camping. Rangers and volunteers hold interpretive programs, bird and flower walks, hikes, and campfire programs.

Concessions: Lake Perris has boat moorings, ramps, and boat rentals; biking, hiking, and horseback-riding trails in the hills; and grocery and supply stores. The campground has 167 tent sites and 265 RV sites with hookups, and must be reserved in advance. A primitive horse camp has corrals, water troughs, picnic tables, fire rings, water, and chemical toilets. This park is busy, so call before coming.

Pets: Allowed on leashes only. $1 per day, as in all California state parks.

For more information:

  California State Park Regional Headquarters, 909-657-0676.

  Lake Perris campground, 909-657-9000.

CHINO HILLS STATE PARK

During the days of the Mexican Californios and the great Spanish land-grant ranchos, most of Southern California's inland valleys and rolling hills were forested with ancient oaks and watered by meandering streams.

At 11,000-acre Chino Hills, one of the newest state parks and a former ranch in the hills north of Santa Ana Canyon, you can get an idea of the original appearance of most of lowland Southern California. Broad, grassy hills roll away to the horizon, bright green in the weeks following a rain, and gold fading to brown in late summer and fall.

At Chino Hills, a biological island in a sea of rapidly growing urbanization, stands of ancient oaks grow on the hills, and tall sycamores, recognizable by their scaly white and tan bark, shade the banks of seasonal creeks. One of the last large stands of California black walnut, a native tree, also grows here.

Rangers report the presence of deer, coyotes, rabbits, ground squirrels, and other small mammals, and occasional sightings of badgers and bobcats. Thirty miles of multiuse trails are open to hikers, bikers, and horseback riders. Because there are several equestrian campsites with corrals, the area is a favorite destination for riders who trailer their horses for weekend outings. Mountain-bike riding is also on the rise here.

Where: The park is on the Los Angeles–Orange County line, south of Pomona. The entrance is on Pomona-Rincon Road, 4.5 miles north of the junction of State 71 and State 91.
Hours: No limit.
Admission: Free for daytime use; charge for overnight camping.
Best time to visit: Spring, early summer, late fall. Late summers may be smoggy.
Activities: Hiking, equestrian camping and riding, picnicking, studying the flora and fauna of oak lowlands, bird-watching.
Concessions: A small visitors center with exhibits. Camping in eight primitive sites.
Pets: Allowed on leashes.
For more information:
   Chino Hills State Park, 714-780-6222.

3

Central Coast
and Inland Valleys

The central coast and inland valleys north of Los Angeles are
spread over four big counties — Ventura, Santa Barbara, San Luis
Obispo, and Kern — with a total land area of 6,104 square miles,
about the same size as New Hampshire and Vermont together.
But the population is still relatively small, hence the area's parks
and forests tend to be less crowded than those south of the city.

As almost everywhere in Southern California, mountains
define the region. Here they form the coastal range, which begins near the border of Los Angeles and Ventura Counties and
follows the shoreline in a northwest direction, trapping fog and
moisture on the Pacific side and creating semiarid conditions on
the inland slopes.

Though geologists talk of the coastal range as if it were a
single mountain chain, it's actually made up of waves of small
ranges carved by deep canyons and punctuated by stony peaks.
Most of these ranges lie within Los Padres National Forest
boundaries. With a climate tempered by the ocean and elevations

ranging from sea level to 8,831 feet, the forest is accessible year-round for recreation.

San Joaquin Valley (the lower half of Central Valley) is east of the mountains in Santa Barbara and San Luis Obispo Counties, a land marked by weathered canyons and semiarid flatland. With irrigation, the valley is a breadbasket for the nation; without water, little will grow. But this great inland basin was not always so water-dependent.

Before 1850, San Joaquin Valley was a marshy flood plain, renewed continually by hundreds of small rivers flowing from surrounding mountains. After the 1849 gold rush, when settlers began to arrive, the marshes were drained for farming and the rivers dammed and channeled, destroying a rich and fertile habitat that had supported thousands of animals and countless birds.

LOS PADRES NATIONAL FOREST

Steep, inaccessible canyons, rocky peaks, weathered pinnacles, seasonal streams, and dense forests—this is Los Padres National Forest, California's second largest, with 1,962,700 acres within its boundaries.

The forest was created to protect the watershed of the coastal ranges—Santa Lucia, Garcia, La Panza, Sierra Madre, Santa Ynez, and San Rafael—mountains that zigzag west and northwest, rearing up to form a spectacular backdrop behind towns such as Oxnard, Ventura, and Santa Barbara.

The mountains are higher in the south and get progressively lower toward the northwest; elevations range from near sea level to 8,831 feet on the top of Mount Pinos. The national forest is divided into three regions; the lower two, the ones discussed in this chapter, are the largest. The third region, in Monterey County to the north, is beyond Southern California—not just geographically, but in spirit—and thus is not included in this book.

The land: Los Padres National Forest is a "land of contrasts." This surprising diversity of terrain and climate is caused partly by elevation differences and partly by variations in annual rainfall, which measures from eight to sixty inches, depending on location. More than 500 miles of creeks and rivers drain the mountains, reaching flood proportions during the rainy season (December through May) and slowing to a trickle in September.

Almost forty-eight percent of Los Padres National Forest has now been included in ten wilderness areas (eight are described in the next section), and the process of conservation is ongoing. In 1992 alone, 400,450 roadless acres were reclassified as wilderness. According to forest rangers, still more sections have been identified for future wilderness designation.

A portion of one wilderness, the Sespe Condor Sanctuary in the southeast national forest, is reserved for the protection of the California condor, North America's largest bird and an endangered species. The condor, once seen frequently soaring over most of Southern California, is now being raised in captivity for reintroduction to the Sespe, its last native habitat. Hunters, power lines, and poisoned bait are the condor's chief enemies.

Wildlife: Because so much of the forest is remote and impenetrable, animals and plants less conspicuous than the condor do continue to thrive. The list of 468 identified birds and animals includes not only the condor, but the American peregrine falcon, southern bald eagle, wild turkey, San Joaquin kit fox, black bear, mountain lion, bobcat, and wild pig, plus various species of bats and rattlesnakes. Sixteen species of fish live in year-round streams; one trout species is native to Los Padres.

A list of identified trees includes coast live oak, coastal redwoods, Douglas fir, white fir, rare bristlecone fir, and limber, pinyon, Jeffrey, ponderosa, Coulter, sugar, and knobcone pines. Poison oak, the picnickers' bane, is common.

Recreation: Although 1,200 miles of hiking and horseback-riding trails make most wilderness areas accessible,

California condor

backpackers are only a fraction of the total number of visitors. Day hikers and car campers are the main recreationists, and they stay nearer the perimeter, close to the forest's 106 campgrounds.

Nineteen organizations operate camps on weekends and during the summer (including the Boy Scouts, the Girl Scouts, the YMCA, and church groups), over the years giving many local residents their first youthful introduction to the wilderness experience.

Less widely known forest attractions include seven hot springs—four on public land and three on private land within forest boundaries. For directions to Big Caliente (the only developed spring) and Little Caliente, contact the Santa Barbara District office; for Sespe Hot Springs, contact the Ojai District office; and for Sykes Hot Springs, contact the Monterey District office.

Matilija Hot Springs (Ojai District), Tassajara Hot Springs (Monterey District), and the Esalan Institute (Monterey District) are private spas for which reservations are required.

To hike or backpack in any of the wilderness areas, you must obtain a free permit. Fire permits aren't needed in developed campgrounds, but are required elsewhere. Most, but not all, campgrounds are improved with piped water, pit toilets, tables, and grills. The general rule is, the farther from the road, the more primitive.

Forest fires are a threat in late summer and early fall, particularly after a dry winter. If the weather is unusually hot and dry, certain sections of the forest may be closed to all activities.

Where: Road access is from any state or county road along the forest borders. Main roads are Gibraltar Road and Camino Cielo near Santa Barbara; Figueroa Mountain and Happy Canyon Road in Santa Inez Valley; Tepusquet Road near Santa Maria.
Hours: No limit.
Admission: Free for daytime use and backpacking. Developed campgrounds charge $7 to $11 per night.

Best time to visit: Spring, summer, and fall before the fire season.

Activities: Hiking, backpacking, nature walks, bird-watching, animal identification, picnicking. Auto-club county maps, topographical maps, or Forest Service maps are recommended for all hiking and car trips.

Concessions: Don't rely on finding markets or stores. Bring all your food, water and supplies.

Pets: Allowed on leashes.

For more information:

Los Padres National Forest Supervisor, 6144 Calle Real, Goleta, CA 93117; 805-683-6711.

Mount Pinos Ranger District, Star Route, Box 400, Frazier Park, CA 93225; 805-245-3731.

Ojai Ranger District, 1190 East Ojai Avenue, Ojai, CA 93023; 805-646-4348.

Santa Barbara Ranger District, Star Route, Los Prietos, Santa Barbara, CA 93105; 805-967-3481.

Santa Lucia Ranger District, 1616 Carlotti Drive, Santa Maria, CA 93454; 805-925-9538.

LOS PADRES NATIONAL FOREST WILDERNESS AREAS

In 1992, some wilderness areas were enlarged and new ones were created. Though some unmaintained dirt fire roads may remain, they're closed to motorized vehicles. Hiking, backpacking, and horseback riding are the only ways to reach the interior.

Dozens of campgrounds are located at the ends of paved and dirt roads and along trails in the interior. No matter where you want to hike, you'll find one or more camping areas nearby.

Good maps are important, not only to stay on trails, but to find trailheads and the roads that access them. Bring a library of county, Forest Service, and topographical maps; it's been our experience that no single map shows everything you want to know, including the trails, roads, campgrounds, topographical features, and boundaries of parks, wilderness areas, and counties.

Sespe Wilderness, southeast Ventura County: This very large wilderness, 219,000 acres, is west and north of the Sespe Condor Sanctuary (described above), where biologists are releasing birds raised in captivity. If you're lucky, you may see one soaring overhead.

Hiking trails begin from Beaver Campground, off State 33, a paved road, from paved roads north of Ojai, and from paved roads directly west of Hungry Valley State Vehicular Recreation Area, off I-5 north of Pyramid Lake.

Chumash Wilderness, northeast Ventura County, west of Frazier Park: This small wilderness, 38,158 acres on the north slope of the Pine Mountains, is accessible from Potrero Road and hiking trails connecting 8,286-foot Mount Abel and 8,831-foot Mount Pinos, the highest point in the range.

If you can arrange a pickup, take one of our favorite day trips: a one-way hike from the summit of one mountain to the summit of the other, a seven-mile trip through remote and beautiful valleys.

The parking lot and trailhead at Mount Abel are on the summit. At Mount Pinos, park in the lot below the top and climb up the old road (now closed to traffic), about 1.5 miles to the summit, the trailhead, and a magnificent and panoramic view of the wilderness.

Matilija Wilderness, southwest Ventura County, northeast of Carpenteria: Creeks, canyons, and wildflowers are the fare in this 29,600-acre wilderness in the Santa Inez mountains north of Lake Casitas. Trails into the area begin at various points along State 33: at the end of Matilija Dam Road; in Wheeler Gorge; and from several spots farther north on State 33, as far as the Pine Mountain Inn.

Dick Smith Wilderness, east border of Santa Barbara

County: The Dick Smith and San Rafael Wildernesses, deep in the heart of the national forest, are a playground for Santa Barbara to the south. A few national-forest trails head toward Dick Smith's 64,000 acres from paved roads in the canyons north of Santa Barbara, but in most places, the wilderness borders are miles beyond, a long way from national-forest borders.

Trails that do enter the wilderness, where its boundaries are close to the forest's boundaries, begin at Lower Buckhorn Campground, directly north of downtown Santa Barbara and off State 33, on the wilderness's east border.

San Rafael Wilderness, east-central Santa Barbara County: Paved roads into the canyons behind Santa Barbara and Lake Cachuma lead to trails into this 195,570-acre wilderness, the first area given National Wilderness status, in 1968. The most direct access to the backcountry is the trail from Potrero Campground off County 3350 and Sunset Valley Road, which connects directly to the other major trails along the crest.

Other popular hikes on national-forest trails outside wilderness boundaries are the 4.5-mile Springs Trail to East Camino Cielo; the Davy Brown Trail from Figueroa Mountain through Fir Canyon to Davy Brown Campground; the five-mile Little Pine Mountain Trail from Upper Oso Campground to the 4,506-foot Pine Mountain; and the six-mile McPherson Peak Trail, from Aliso Campground on the north slope of the Sierra Madre Mountains to the summit of 5,749-foot McPherson Peak.

Santa Lucia Wilderness, in the Santa Lucia Range, east of the town of San Luis Obispo: The 21,678-acre Santa Lucia Wilderness, about eighteen miles long and 3.5 miles across at its widest point, is a narrow section of land crowning the summit of the Santa Lucia Mountains east of San Luis Obispo.

These are rocky, dry mountains, with chaparral vegetation and a riparian habitat along year-round creeks. Elevations range from about 750 to 3,000 feet. Trails begin in canyons off Lopez

Canyon Road and Forest Road 30S11, and from Forest Road 30S05, on the east side of the mountains.

Garcia Wilderness, in the Garcia Mountains, east of the Santa Lucia Wilderness: This 14,100-acre wilderness is directly east of the Santa Lucia Wilderness and shares the same climate and vegetation. Trails start on the south side of County M3094, from Stony Creek Campground, and from the end of several dirt roads near the base of the mountains.

Machesne Mountain Wilderness, in the La Panza Mountains, east of the Garcia Wilderness: The Machesne Mountain Wilderness, on the east side of the Garcia Mountains, comprises 20,000 acres around 4,054-foot Machesne Mountain. Forest Road 16E02 is the main trailhead feeding into a network of trails across the mountains from Pine Spring Camp.

The road to American Canyon, off County M3094, which looks like a good approach route on the map, is actually a private lane on Avenales Ranch and is closed to vehicles. One way to climb Machesne Mountain is to walk up American Canyon, a twelve-mile hike to the summit from here. Bear in mind that you're on private land. A rutted dirt road rises from Castle Crags on the north side, leading to a shorter trail up Mount Machesne, but the road is passable for four-wheel-drive vehicles only.

Where: In Los Padres National forest, in Ventura, Santa Barbara, and San Luis Obispo Counties.
Hours: No limit.
Admission: No fee to hike; camping fees charged separately.
Best time to visit: Late winter, spring, and summer.
Activities: Hiking, backpacking, mountain biking, fishing, camping, bird-watching.
Concessions: None.
Pets: Not allowed in wilderness areas.
For more information:
   Los Padres National Forest Supervisor, 6144 Calle Real, Goleta, CA 93117; 805-683-6711.

Mount Pinos Ranger District, Star Route, Box 400, Frazier Park, CA 93225; 805-245-3731.

Ojai Ranger District, 1190 East Ojai Avenue, Ojai, CA 93023; 805-646-4348.

Santa Barbara Ranger District, Star Route, Los Prietos, Santa Barbara, CA 93105; 805-967-3481.

Santa Lucia Ranger District, 1616 Carlotti Drive, Santa Maria, CA 93454; 805-925-9538.

LAKE PIRU RECREATION AREA

This man-made lake, which captures runoff from Piru Creek and the mountains to the north, was intended for powerboat recreation; hence most visitors are motorboat enthusiasts and water-skiers. Fishing is also good, so bring an ice chest and prepare to fill it with bass, crappie, catfish, and trout.

The lake, at 1,000 feet elevation in rolling, arid hills, is in Ventura County, at the southernmost border between Angeles and Los Padres National Forests. The Sespe Condor Sanctuary is directly west, and campers have been known to spend many hours looking through binoculars, hoping to sight the twelve-foot wingspan of the nearly extinct bird.

There are two campgrounds on the west shore. Olive Grove is our favorite, especially in late winter, when few campers are out, the lakeside is quiet, the weather is sunny and mild, and you can have the place to yourself. Ramps, moorings, and slips are available for boaters; boats under twelve feet aren't allowed on the lake.

Where: Six miles northeast of Piru and east of Fillmore, off State 126 and Piru Canyon Road, in Ventura County.
Hours: 8:30 A.M. to dusk, except for campers.
Admission: $5 per vehicle entry fee. No extra charges to use the paved boat ramp, temporary moorings, and slips.

Best time to visit: Year-round.
Activities: Fishing, waterskiing, pleasure boating, camping.
Concessions: A concessionaire rents motorboats and water skis, and sells tackle, bait, groceries, and general supplies. Meals available at a small café.
Pets: Allowed on leashes.
For more information:
    Lake Piru Recreation Area, P.O. Box 202, Piru, CA 93040; 805-521-1500.

LAKE CASITAS

Ventura County's biggest recreation lake, 2,700-acre Lake Casitas, in the foothills north of the city of Ventura, is an ideal location for a family campout, with the county's largest campground, excellent fishing, boat ramps, and boat rentals. In addition, once-a-month special events are staged here, offering an entirely different dimension to weekend recreation.

Recent events included a Civil War encampment, with participants in period costume using authentic nineteenth-century camp equipment; a Native American powwow, with dancers in costume and the opportunity to buy original art; and a wine festival, with local wineries participating in tastings.

Since Lake Casitas, which has thirty-one miles of shoreline, is a man-made reservoir for Ventura County's drinking water, swimming, waterskiing, and windsurfing aren't allowed. But you can sail, motorboat or row; motorboats, rowboats, and paddle boats are available for rent at the marina.

The campground has 450 sites, some along the water and some farther inland under the oak trees. One hundred forty sites have full RV hookups; the others have tables, grills, and running water. Showers are in a central bathhouse. Sites can be reserved.

Because the lake is easy to reach, it's popular with local

fishermen. Parents teaching children to fish, and children catching the big ones, are common sights. Expect to find a perch, a bass, or a trout on your hook; the lake is stocked regularly. The bait and tackle shop sells the usual supplies.

Most anglers own or rent a boat so that they can get out to deep water. But if you'd rather cast from the shore, ask for a campsite in the "F" loop, which runs next to the water. The "B" loop, along a bluff, has spectacular lake views. Quiet hours are in effect from 10:00 P.M. to 7:00 A.M.

Where: Fourteen miles north of Ventura between State 33 and State 150, in Ventura County.
Hours: Daytime use or overnight camping.
Admission: Daytime use is $5 per car. Campsites run from $12 to $20, depending on location and date. Boat entry fees are $4.
Best time to visit: Year-round.
Activities: Pleasure boating, camping, fishing, monthly special events. For campsite reservations call 805-649-1122. The reservationist knows the campground and can help you pick an appropriate site. Boat rentals, 805-649-2043.
Concessions: Market, bait and tackle store, full snack bar.
Pets: Allowed on leashes.
For more information:
    Lake Casitas, 11311 Santa Ana Road, Ventura, CA 93001; 805-649-2233.

LAKE CACHUMA COUNTY PARK

For years, people have known that Lake Cachuma, a popular recreation lake and man-made reservoir on the Santa Ynez River northwest of Santa Barbara, was a good place to catch fish. Recently, however, bald eagles migrating from the Pacific Northwest, Canada, and Alaska have made the same discovery. The result? Lake Cachuma is now the best place in Southern California to see bald eagles.

Each year from November through February, bald eagles congregate in the trees along the lake's forty-two miles of shoreline to hunt large schools of trout that feed near the surface.

California Department of Fish and Game biologists, who stock the lake with 150,000 rainbow trout from September through March, say that the eagles originally followed migrating waterfowl (also an important part of their diet) to the lake, but now eat primarily trout. Last year, for the first time since the lake was filled in 1958, a pair of eagles stayed on through the summer.

Excursion boats conduct "eagle cruises" on the lake between November and February, taking passengers in search of the thirty- to forty-inch-long raptors and approaching to within 200 yards of their roosting sites. The cruises sell out quickly, so call for reservations.

From March through October, "wildlife cruises" ply the waters in search of other birds and animals. Ranger naturalists have identified some 274 other bird species near the lake, including great blue herons, ospreys, red-tailed hawks, acorn woodpeckers, mallard and ruddy ducks, snow geese, tundra swans, grebes, turkey vultures, quail, owls, loons, hummingbirds, egrets, kingfishers, and orioles.

On shore, rangers conduct nature programs, nature walks, campfire talks, and astronomy programs. The visitors center has natural-history and geology exhibits.

A campground and services are adjacent to the lake (which is owned and operated by Santa Barbara County). Developed sites for tents and RVs, hookups, tables, grills, showers, and even horse corrals are provided. One of Santa Barbara County's most cherished camping rules governs noise: radios, tape players, generators, and things that go bump in the night aren't permitted between 10:00 P.M. and 7:00 A.M.

Nearby are stores, a gas station, a laundromat, a snack

bar and grill, children's play areas, and two swimming pools. Because Lake Cachuma is used for county drinking water, body-contact sports—including swimming, windsurfing, and water-skiing—aren't allowed.

Launch ramps and mooring tie-ups are available for sail-boats and motorboats; canoes and rowboats over ten feet are also allowed. You can rent boats and tackle. In addition to trout, the catch includes bass, catfish, bluegills, crappie, and red-eared perch.

Where: On State 154 north of Santa Barbara, in Santa Barbara County.

Hours: Daytime use, 6:00 A.M. to 10:00 P.M., and overnight camping.

Admission: $3.50 per car for daytime use. Camping fees are $12 per car; RV hookups start at $16 per night. Weekly and senior rates available. Boats are $3.50 per day. Hot showers, twenty-five cents for three minutes.

Best time to visit: Year-round. November through March is best for trout fishing and bird-watching.

Activities: Pleasure boating, fishing, bird-watching, camping, bicycling, summer movies, picnicking, nature activities; children's play facilities available. For group camp reservations, call 805-688-4658; fishing report, 805-688-7724; eagle-cruise reservations, 805-568-2460.

Concessions: Supply store, food market, laundromat, boat rentals, bike rentals, showers. Five hundred campsites (tents and RVs) are issued on a first-come first-served basis. There are six horse sites with corrals.

Pets: Allowed on leashes; not allowed in boats or within fifty feet of the shore.

For more information:

Lake Cachuma, Star Route, Highway 154, Santa Barbara, CA 93105; 805-688-8780.

CHANNEL ISLANDS NATIONAL PARK

Channel Islands National Park, five rocky and virtually unin-
habited islets west of Point Mugu and about twelve miles south of
the Santa Barbara coast, isn't a destination for the faint of heart.

If your main interest in the Channel Islands is to see and
photograph large marine mammals—seals and sea lions on their
home turf—consider taking a half- or full-day excursion by boat
from Ventura Harbor.

But for the intrepid outdoorsman willing to plan, organize,
work like a packhorse, and stay cheerful on a rugged camping
expedition, a memorable adventure awaits you.

The rocky coast of 10,000-acre San Miguel, the westernmost island, is the mating grounds of the California and stellar
sea lion, the harbor and northern elephant seal, northern fur seal,
and the Guadalupe fur seal. Santa Rosa's 55,000 acres include
grassy inland valleys, a forest of threatened Torrey pines, and
fossil dwarf-mammoth bones. Little 640-acre Anacapa is known
for its pristine tidepools; Santa Barbara, also 640 acres in size, is
a vast sea-bird rookery. The largest island, 62,000-acre Santa
Cruz, has huge sea caves and mountains to 2,400 feet elevation.

Despite their isolation, the Channel Islands have had a
checkered history since 1542, when Juan Cabrillo, a navigator in
the service of the Spanish viceroy in Mexico, first hauled out on
the shores of San Miguel.

Over the following 400 years, ranchers, farmers, fur
traders, fishermen, and munitions testers used these islands,
altering plant and animal communities and damaging native
habitats. The islands, which some experts believe are the sub-
merged tips of the Santa Monica Mountains, have been separated
from the mainland for so long that several unique plant and
animal species have evolved.

The cycle of exploitation and commercial use continued
until 1938, when President Franklin D. Roosevelt designated

Young elephant seals

Anacapa and Santa Barbara national monuments. In 1976, San Miguel was transferred to National Park Service management, and in 1980, President Jimmy Carter created Channel Islands National Park. Later that year, a six-mile perimeter around the five islands was drawn, establishing a national marine sanctuary underwater.

The only transportation to the islands is by boat—your private vessel or a chartered excursion boat. Expect a choppy crossing and, upon landing, either a plunge through roiling surf as you carry your gear above your head, or a long climb up a steel ladder (also while carrying your gear), followed by a half-mile hike to the campground.

Except for limited rustic ranch accommodations on Santa Cruz (see below), overnight visitors must bring all their own food, water, stoves, tents, fuel, and warm clothes for camping. There are no supplies, stores, or buildings open to the public.

The camp sites are small (to limit impact on the islands) and without shade or wind protection. Although some days are sunny, the weather is unpredictable; calm, warm days may be followed by periods of wind, fog, or rain.

"It is a harsh environment at best, and a hostile and unforgiving one at its worst," the *National Park Camping Information* brochure warns prospective visitors, noting that you can't "pack up and go home" on a moment's notice.

You may swim, scuba dive, or snorkel only in designated areas and hike only on marked trails. The rangers lead guided interpretive hikes of varying lengths.

Before planning a day or overnight trip, visit the Channel Islands National Park Visitors Center, in Oxnard, where interpretive exhibits and films on the islands' history, geology, habitats, and land and marine animals give you a better idea of what to expect.

The rangers issue visitor and camping permits and distribute maps, rules for visiting, suggestions on what to bring, and information about the Island Packers Company, the concessionaire that conducts trips to all islands except Santa Cruz. (Arrange a trip to this private island through the Santa Barbara Museum of Natural History.)

Santa Cruz was privately owned by several ranching families until 1987. Now four-fifths of the island is managed by the Nature Conservancy and one-fifth by the National Park Service. Guests can stay at Scorpion Ranch at the island's east end, or at historic Christy Ranch at the west end, now used as guest quarters and a field-study station operated by the museum.

Where: South of Santa Barbara and west of Point Mugu.

Hours: The visitors center in Oxnard is open daily, except for holidays, during normal business hours. On the islands, campers are restricted to campground areas at night.

Admission: Permits are free. Transportation and tours are priced through Island Packers. Half-day trips to Anacapa are $21; full-day trips are $37 to $62 for adults, less for seniors and children. A two-day excursion to San Miguel and Santa Rosa, with five meals and ship's berth, is $215 per person.

Best time to visit: Summer and fall are warmest and sunniest; the water is also much warmer between June and September. Late winter and spring may be rainy or foggy, with cold water.

Activities: Camping, hiking, bird-watching, scuba diving, snorkeling, and animal observation.

Concessions: Rates at Christy Ranch vary according to date and the number of guests. Contact Christy Ranch, Santa Barbara Museum of Natural History, 2559 Puesta del Sol Road, Santa Barbara, CA 93105; 805-682-4711. For Scorpion Ranch, contact Island Packers, 1867 Spinnaker Drive, Ventura, CA 93001; 805-642-1393.

Pets: Not allowed.

For more information:

Channel Islands National Park, Visitors Center, 1901 Spinnaker Drive, Ventura, CA 93001; 805-658-5730.

VENTURA COUNTY STATE BEACHES

Three of Ventura County's many beaches are part of the California State Park system, and two of the three have campgrounds. While many of the campers and weekenders taking advantage of these miles of unspoiled white sand are local folks, the beaches are excellent stopover points for travelers driving along the coast.

To be assured of a campsite, make reservations through MISTIX (800-444-7275), more than a week in advance. Unreserved sites are issued on the spot on a first-come first-served basis.

McGrath State Beach: If you're camping at McGrath, ask for a campsite on the crest of the dunes above this two-mile stretch of beach west of Oxnard. It's windier on the dunes than on the grass among the trees, but the views of the ocean and the distant Channel Islands are unforgettable.

Nearby is the mouth of the Santa Clara River and a protected estuary for marine birds and animals. To see the marshes up close, follow a nature trail through the dunes and willows.

Swimming, bodysurfing, and fishing are good at any point along the beach. But watch out for riptides, which form occasionally in spots where the ocean bottom drops steeply or unevenly away from the beach. If you get caught in a riptide, which is a narrow river of water flowing out to sea between incoming waves, swim parallel to the shore to escape.

McGrath's 174 developed campsites are grouped around a grassy park and a supply store. RVs up to thirty-four feet are allowed.

San Buenaventura State Beach: There are glorious ocean views from the 1,700-foot-long pier at San Buenaventura State Beach. On the beach itself, you can swim, wade on the sandy bottom, or sun yourself behind one of several rock jetties, which create small coves and form bulwarks against the wind.

Inland, the rocky summits of the coastal range rise against the sky. A two-mile bike path starts here and travels west past the town of Ventura and the Channel Islands National Park Visitors Center to Emma Wood State Beach. There are summer lifeguards, 165 picnic sites, and 1,200 parking spaces at this beach, but no campsites. The snack bar and bait shop are currently closed and awaiting new owners.

Emma Wood State Beach: For years, Ventura County has operated the campground at Emma Wood as a primitive facility, with no tables, water, or toilets. But because no reservations are needed to camp at these sites, which are filled on a first-come first-served basis, Emma Wood is a popular overnight place for travelers who find themselves in the area at dusk without a place to stay.

Campers who stay more than one night can swim, fish, or surf. The beach is part rock and part sand. The bike path from San Buenaventura has been extended recently, so bicycle riders can continue west to Rincon Point and Rincon Beach and County Park (a surfing hangout famous for great waves), just south of the town of Carpenteria.

Where: In Ventura County, west of Oxnard and Ventura. McGrath is off Harbor Boulevard; San Buenaventura and Emma Wood are off US 101.

Hours: No limit. Check in at reserved campgrounds during daylight hours.

Admission: No fee for daytime use. Overnight camping is $14 per vehicle in winter, $16 in summer.

Best time to visit: Beautiful year-round. Warm in summer, cool and windy in winter. Fog likely between March and June.

Activities: Swimming, bicycling, surfing, fishing, camping.

Concessions: None.

Pets: $1 extra; allowed on leashes; not allowed on beaches.
For more information:
McGrath and San Buenaventura State Beaches, 805-899-1400.
Emma Wood State Beach, 805-654-3951.
MISTIX reservations, 800-444-7275.

SANTA BARBARA COUNTY STATE BEACHES

Four state beaches in Santa Barbara County, between Carpenteria in the east and Point Conception in the west, where the coast swings north, depend on their southern orientation and warm ocean waters for some of the best swimming and fishing in the region.

Despite the perception that California's coastline runs north and south, a look at the map shows that between Santa Barbara and Point Conception, it runs east and west. East of Point Conception, where the following beaches are located, ocean waters are protected and relatively warm, with temperatures ranging from the low 60s in winter to about 74 in summer. North of Point Conception, the cold Pacific current sweeps past, making the water temperatures, even in summer, too cold for comfortable swimming.

Carpenteria State Beach: This one-mile beach, just south of the town of Carpenteria, is long, wide, and flat, a good place to wiggle your toes in the sand, wade, dig clams, or introduce toddlers to the waves. At low tide, pools in offshore rocks invite you to look (but not collect).

Joggers invariably come away with stubborn black tar spots on their feet—not the effects of oil drilling, but a souvenir of the natural tar pits below ground, which ooze into the ocean and wash onshore.

The Chumash people, who lived in the area and paddled

their canoes far out to sea, built their boats on the shore, using tar to caulk the bottoms. When the Spanish arrived after 1769, they saw the Chumash hollowing out huge logs for canoes and named the area *Carpenteria*, or "carpentry shop."

Scuba divers like Carpenteria's offshore rock formations, while surfers head for fabled Rincon Point, three miles east, where daily swells average two to four feet and grow to twelve feet after a major winter storm.

**Curlews' long bills are useful for grabbing beetles
and other tasty invertebrates**

Lifeguards patrol this beach in summer. The large camp-ground is a good destination for families, and convenient for sight-seeing in Santa Barbara. It's off State 224, twelve miles east of Santa Barbara.

El Capitan State Beach: For years, some friends of ours who are avid fishermen celebrated Thanksgiving weekend at El Capitan State Beach, fifteen miles west of Santa Barbara. The holiday began on Thursday, when they roasted a turkey in a covered barbecue, and ended Sunday morning, after a lavish Saturday-night fresh-fish fry.

An elaborate menu, perhaps, for campers, but our friends are regulars at El Capitan – people who camp here time and time again, claiming that this state beach, the Southland's most scenic cove, is the only place to spend an important holiday.

Stands of stately old sycamores and oaks line the banks of El Capitan Creek, climbing the hills to the tops of the bluffs. A bike path heads west for 2.5 miles to Refugio State Beach. A pathway down the hill connects the tops of the bluffs to the beach, and to good swimming coves and rocky tidepools. The surf fishing is good for barred perch, cabezon, calico bass, and halibut.

Occasionally you'll sight sea lions, seals, and gray whales swimming offshore. During the summer months, rangers lead nature hikes and conduct campfire and junior nature programs.

The campground has 140 sites for tents and RVs, with tables, fire rings, pay hot showers, and restrooms. There are no RV hookups. A small market sells supplies, ice, and staples.

In summer, sites are booked weeks in advance; you'll have better luck getting space from October through May. Still, if you're in the vicinity, stop by and check availability – the rangers at the entrance kiosk sometimes get last-minute cancellations. The beach is off US 101, fifteen miles west of Santa Barbara.

Refugio State Beach: If El Capitan is full, Refugio runs a close second for classic good looks and California ambience.

Palm trees sway in the ocean breeze; Refugio Creek burbles down to the ocean; and, beyond the 1.5 miles of beach, Anacapa, Santa Rosa, San Miguel, and Santa Cruz Islands float on the horizon. The palms, incidentally, aren't native to this area, but were planted years ago, before the cove became a park.

The campground is small – part of the park's charm – with eighty-five sites, a market, hot showers, and a laundry. Both tents and RVs are welcome, but there are no hookups. It's on Refugio Road off US 101, 2.5 miles past El Capitan and 17.5 miles west of Santa Barbara.

Gaviota State Park and Beach: The biggest of Santa Barbara's beach parks is Gaviota State Beach and 2,700-acre Gaviota State Park, located at the southwest tip of Los Padres National Forest, where the Santa Ynez Mountains reach the sea and US 101 turns away from the ocean and heads north across Gaviota Pass.

The park and beach surround Gaviota Creek, named by early Spanish explorers for the thousands of seagulls they found near the water. Sand beaches and small coves on the water side are designated for swimming, surf fishing, and picnicking. Boats can be launched with a hoist installed on ramps on the beach. The campground's fifty-four campsites lie beneath shade trees, farther up the canyon along the creek.

Several hiking trails head into the canyons on the mountain side of the park. A rite of passage for all first-time Gaviota campers is the climb to the summit of 2,458-foot Gaviota Peak, just over the national-forest border.

Reservations aren't accepted at Gaviota. RV sites have no facilities or hookups; tent sites have tables, fire pits, showers, and flush toilets.

A word of warning about Gaviota: as is common these days, here and elsewhere around the world, wilderness and industry are uneasy neighbors. Several pipelines transporting oil and sour gas (which contains hydrogen sulfide, a flammable, poisonous chemical) cross sections of park property. Should a leak or a spill occur, says the state-park pamphlet, a warning tone and a message will sound on the recently installed public-address system. Gaviota is off US 101, thirty-one miles west of Santa Barbara.

Where: On the south coast of Santa Barbara County.
Hours: No limit.
Admission: There may be daytime-use fees for cars. Overnight-camping fees are $14 per vehicle in winter and $16 in summer.
Best time to visit: Summer and fall. Spring is foggy; winter is cool and windy.
Activities: Swimming, surfing, surf fishing, scuba diving, beach combing, jogging, camping, biking.
Concessions: Some parks have small stores.
Pets: $1 extra; dogs allowed on leashes, but not allowed on beaches.
For more information:
>   California State Parks, 805-899-1400.
>   MISTIX reservations, 800-444-7275.

LA PURISIMA MISSION STATE HISTORIC PARK

"What strange shoes you're wearing," said Father Juan Martine, peering down at our two-tone nylon tennis shoes. "I don't recognize that material. Here at La Purisima Mission, we wear leather sandals we've made ourselves, of cowhide."

"We also spin wool and weave our own cloth," he continued, indicating his outfit, a heavy brown hooded cassock tied with a rope belt. "We grow all our food in these gardens and build our own furniture of oak. In this wilderness so far from Mexico City, we have to be self-sufficient."

Father Martine, aka Thomas Hacker, a docent at 968-acre

La Purisima Mission State Historic Park near Lompoc, stays in character when he meets time-warp travelers.

In 1787, Franciscan padres founded La Purisima on a 300,000-acre mission land grant in this valley. After the earthquake of 1812 destroyed the church, the padres chose a new building site four miles away across the river (the present location). After Mexican independence, the government abandoned the mission system and the buildings were deserted. By 1900, this and most other California missions had crumbled to ruins.

But in the late 1930s, CCC (Civilian Conservation Corps) work crews began a four-year restoration project. They lived day and night in tents on the site, made adobe bricks of traditional straw and clay, and rebuilt all nine original structures.

Today, every August on "Mission Life Day," costumed docents demonstrate crafts of the 1820s, such as candlemaking, weaving, carpentry, horseshoeing, and brickmaking. Self-guided one-hour tours visit the church (large enough to hold 1,000 people), the carpentry shop, the blacksmith shop, the pottery shop, the gristmill, the tallow vats, the candlemaking shop, the wine press, the weaving room, the springhouse, the barracks, and the kitchen.

In one of the craft shops we paused to watch a docent weave wool cloth on a tall floor loom, then took a turn ourselves. As we struggled to keep the threads taut and even, the docent said that between 1787 and 1812, Chumash weavers made 40,000 such blankets on similar looms, which the mission used for trading with coastal ships.

The mission gardens reflect the period, planted with fruit, trees, shrubs, and herbs including grape, fig, pear, pepper, olive, currant, pomegranates, rosemary, and sage. Two bronze bells in the bell tower (the campanario) were cast in Peru in 1817 and 1818; the wooden bell above them was made by Chumash.

The La Purisima Visitors Center Museum near the park entrance documents the history of the mission and its Chumash converts. Thousands of Chumash and some Spanish soldiers are buried in the cemetery in the manner of the day: hastily and without individual markers. In destroying the Chumash's family groups, the missions also destroyed their culture.

The hills behind the mission host a unique plant community called the Burton Mesa Chaparral, accessible from fourteen miles of hiking and equestrian trails. Even a short walk back into the woods recalls the days before the Spanish arrived, when the country was wild and unspoiled.

Where: Three miles from Lompoc on State 246 and Purisima Road in Santa Barbara County.
Hours: Daily except Thanksgiving, Christmas, and New Year's Day, from 9:00 A.M. to 5:00 P.M.
Admission: $5 per vehicle.
Best time to visit: Year-round. Busiest and warmest in summer. Winter and spring weather may be variable.
Activities: Historic tours and demonstrations by docents in period costume; also exhibits, museum tours, photography, picnicking, hiking, horseback ridiॣ g.
Concessions: No camping or food service; picnic tables are available.
Pets: On leashes; $1 extra.
For more information:
Purisima Mission State Historic Park, 805-733-3713.

PISMO STATE BEACH AND PISMO DUNES STATE VEHICLE RECREATION AREA

Children and surfers in wet suits may be the only people who can stand the cold Pacific waters of San Luis Obispo County, but the parks and campgrounds along the coast, some of the state's most scenic, make up in natural beauty what they lack in recreational swimming.

The rolling sand dunes and six-mile shoreline of Pismo Beach, where local folks once boasted that "anything goes," has now been divided into two areas. One thousand acres of dunes and level beach are reserved for swimmers, sunbathers, beachcombers, surf fishermen, bird-watchers, picnickers, and horseback riders. Another 1,800 acres have been set aside for the activity that made this beach famous: the use of dune buggies and motorized vehicles. The designation of this half of Pismo as an SVRA (State Vehicle Recreation Area) is a recognition that ORVs (off-road vehicles) are here to stay, and that the best strategy for environmental conservation is to provide them with their own dedicated recreational terrain.

But Pismo has earned fame in other ways, as well. Its shifting mounds of sand and broad beaches have served as a set for several movies, not only because the dunes look like something in Saudi Arabia, but because it's legal to drive trucks with heavy equipment over them. For the same reason, Pismo is a great beach for handicapped travelers because a wheelchair user could drive or be driven to the water's edge.

This beach is also famous for "Pismo clams," no longer as plentiful as in the past, but still harvested by local residents. In addition, you can see migrating monarch butterflies in the eucalyptus trees nearby.

There are two campgrounds, one at each end of the state beach, with tent and RV sites, some hookups, showers, and a golf course. You can camp anywhere in the SVRA.

Where: Pismo State Beach is off State 1, two miles south of the town of Pismo Beach. The Dunes SVRA is three miles south of the town, in Oceano.
Hours: No limit.
Admission: No fee. Campsites are $14 to $16 per vehicle and can be reserved.
Best time to visit: May through October. Winter is gorgeous, but cool and windy.

Activities: Driving on the dunes and beach, beachcombing, jogging, fishing, camping, kite flying.
Concessions: In the towns of Pismo Beach and Oceano.
Pets: Allowed on leashes.
For more information:
    Pismo Beach State Park and Dunes SVRA, 805-489-1869 or 805-489-2684 (recorded message).

MONTANA DE ORO STATE PARK

This state park, with rugged inland hills, bluffs, sandy beaches, and spectacular rocky coves washed by the surge of waves and the crash of salt spray, is our candidate for California's wildest and most scenic beach park.

If the water were warmer, the park would be a perfect "ten." But the ocean is very cold. According to Ranger Clay King, water temperatures range from the low 50s in winter to the high 50s in summer, never reaching 60 degrees: as he puts it, "wet-suit water year-round."

On the other hand, the cold, nutrient-bearing Pacific currents support a wonderfully diverse plant and animal community on land and along the shore.

We usually pack a picnic and spend the day here, hiking for a few hours and then beachcombing on the sand and at the water's edge, looking for sea urchins, hermit crabs, and sea cucumbers. At high tide the waves smash on the rocks, shooting plumes of spray into the air and flooding the tidepools.

In the 1960s, Montana de Oro's hidden coves were a hangout for hippies, drawn to many of these secluded and primitive spots. Those same folks, now mostly sober citizens living nearby, bring their children and grandchildren here for the day.

The 8,066-acre park starts at the Morro Bay sandspit and runs south for seven miles along the ocean, with sandy beaches to the north, rocky coves in the center, and bluffs to the south.

The rangers list more than 100 species of birds. Brown pelicans, long on the endangered-species list (DDT in the food chain prevented their eggshells from hardening), nest in the rocks offshore. You may also see sea lions, seals, sea otters, and, in the winter months, migrating California gray whales.

Look for Spooners Cove, where smugglers and bootleggers once plied their trades. The cove is named for the Spooner family, ranchers who owned the land before it became a park. Their former family home on the bluffs is now park headquarters.

Hikers and horseback riders climb the hills behind, through the canyons and along the cliffs on fifty miles of dirt roads and trails. If you're among them, watch for Pacific rattlesnakes, often seen sunning themselves on the trail.

Other animals in the hills are more elusive, but quiet hikers may spot rabbits, gophers, foxes, coyotes, skunks, badgers, bobcats, deer, and even mountain lions. Wildlife biologists estimate that San Luis Obispo County contains the state's largest mountain-lion population, and during recent drought years, they were spotted in town drinking from ponds and creeks.

A four-mile hike climbs to the summit of 1,649-foot Alan Peak, and a half-mile trail in forested Hazard Canyon descends to the beach. The hiking map distributed at the ranger station plots the locations of the trails, which you can combine to make several loop trips.

In spring, when the wildflowers bloom and the hills are a mass of California poppies, daisies, mustard, and fiddleneck, it's easy to see why the Spaniards named the area "Mountains of Gold." The park isn't named for the millions of migrating monarch butterflies, which arrive in Montana de Oro in October and roost in the eucalyptus groves in the hills and along Pecho Valley Road. After resting, some butterflies move on to more southerly climes, but many winter over in the park.

A small campground beside Islay Creek on Pecho Valley Road has fifty tent and RV sites, piped water, pit toilets, tables, and fire rings. RVs up to twenty-four feet are allowed.

Millions of migrating monarchs pass through Southern California

A small campground beside Islay Creek on Pecho Valley Road has fifty tent and RV sites, piped water, pit toilets, tables, and fire rings. RVs up to twenty-four feet are allowed.

Where: Seven miles south of Los Osos, on Pecho Valley Road.
Hours: Daylight, or overnight camping.
Admission: Free for daytime use. Campsites are $7 in winter and $9 in summer. Make reservations with MISTIX, 800-444-7275, for periods between Memorial Day and Labor Day.
Best time to visit: Summer and fall. Spring is changeable, with occasional fog.

Activities: Hiking, camping, bird-watching, marine-animal observation, tidepool visits, photography. Campfires are permitted only in grills or fire rings. There are no lifeguards.

Concessions: None. Supplies available in nearby Los Osos.

Pets: $1 extra; allowed on leashes, but not allowed on trails.

For more information:

Montana de Oro State Park, Los Osos, CA 93402; 805-528-0513.

LOS OSOS OAKS STATE RESERVE

For hundreds of years, stately old oaks with massive crowns shaded the grassy inland hills and valleys of Southern California. Now many of them are gone. Los Osos Oaks State Reserve, a small, eighty-five-acre preserve west of San Luis Obispo, was created to protect one of the last, oldest, and strangest stands of California's coast live oaks, a forest of dwarfed and gnarled 700-year-old trees that have adapted to sandy, nutrient-poor soil.

The Native American tribes of the Central Coast thrived on the bounty of the oaks, gathering and grinding acorns for a nutritious cooked mush. After the Spaniards arrived, many of the trees were harvested for firewood or timber.

The real threat to the oaks, however, occurred after World War II, when people looking for a better life began moving to California. Ironically, many home developers tried to save the mighty trees, leaving them undisturbed wherever possible. Shade trees were considered an asset that enhanced property values. But when the oaks began to die, landscapers realized that while they thrived in hot, dry hills, they soon succumbed to overwatering on suburban lawns.

In another ironic twist, the name of this park—Los Osos Oaks—also salutes another giant now extinct in California: the grizzly bear. During the mission days there were so many grizzlies in the hills near San Luis Obispo that early diaries and letters were full of stories about sightings and encounters. The grizzlies, of course, are long gone.

A one-mile self-guided nature trail winds through the oak groves, offering a chance to experience these noble giants close-up. Be sure to bring a camera.

Where: Off Los Osos Valley Road, northeast of Montana de Oro, about twelve miles west of San Luis Obispo.
Hours: No limit.
Admission: No fees.
Best time to visit: Year-round. Spring flowers from late February through April.
Activities: Viewing, bird-watching, nature walks. Campfires must be in grills or fire rings.
Concessions: None. A parking area is at the entrance.
Pets: Allowed on leashes, but not allowed on trails.
For more information:
Los Osos Oaks State Reserve, 805-528-0513.

MORRO BAY STATE PARK
AND MORRO STRAND STATE BEACH

Along the coast west of San Luis Obispo, where the shore is ragged with high cliffs and rocky coves, Morro Strand State Beach's three-mile expanse, just north of the town of Morro Bay, is a welcome stretch of sand.

In the bay itself, the main landmark is Morro Rock, a plug-dome volcanic cone that erupted twenty-three million years ago and now looms 578 feet above the water at the bay's north end. Morro Rock is also an occasional hazard, and once in a while a sailor lost in a dense winter fog runs into it.

The town of Morro Bay, a patchwork of private homes, cottages, stores, boatyards, and marinas, dots the bay's north shore. Baywood Park, a residential area, is on the south shore. Though commercial fishing is still important in Morro Bay, seaside recreation is now the main activity, and you'll see as many pleasure craft at their moorings as fishing boats.

Morro Bay State Park, 1,960 acres directly east of the bay in low coastal hills, is a combination of developed recreation and natural habitat, with an eighteen-hole golf course, a campground, a picnic area, hiking trails, a natural history museum at White's Point, and a protected estuary.

This large marsh, say biologists, is one of California's last unspoiled coastal wetlands, where brackish water fosters a unique intertidal habitat for crabs, clams, snails, microscopic organisms, fingerling halibut and perch, and dozens of resident and migratory birds. You can canoe through the estuary; rentals are available at the marina.

A blue-heron rookery where the birds mate and nest between February and July—one of the last few on the southern Pacific Coast—is in a grove of eucalyptus trees north of the museum. Great egrets also nest in the area, which is closed to the public. You can see both rookeries from points nearby; binoculars are recommended.

There are two campgrounds in the area, one at Morro State Beach and one at the park. A popular trail climbs to the top of Black Rock, 661 feet high, one of a group of volcanic cones called the Seven Sisters. The museum, open daily except on holidays, has interpretive displays, natural-history exhibits, and artifacts left by the area's first Native American residents. Guided nature walks start at the museum.

Where: Off State 1 in the town of Morro Bay, in San Luis Obispo County.
Hours: Daytime use and overnight camping.

Admission: Fee for parking and camping. No walk-in fee.
Best time to visit: Spring and summer.
Activities: Nature walks, bird-watching, beach sports, fishing.
Concessions: Boat rentals, fishing tackle, groceries, gas, and motels are available in the town.
Pets: Allowed on leashes.
For more information:

Morro Bay State Park, State Park Road, Morro Bay, CA 93442; 805-772-2560, or 805-772-2694 (recorded message).

Museum, 805-772-7434.

LOPEZ LAKE RECREATION AREA

Lopez Lake, in Lopez Canyon on the west slope of the Santa Lucia Mountains, is San Luis Obispo County's most conveniently located recreation lake, and hence the busiest. The 974-acre lake and surrounding county park occupy a total of 4,276 acres nestled in grassy, oak-shaded hills.

Like most man-made lakes in canyons blocked by dams, Lopez is shaped like a "U," with twenty-two miles of shoreline and two irregular, ragged arms. Since the lake is part of a flood-control and irrigation project and swimming is allowed, most visitors are families.

Other water sports on the lake include waterskiing, sailing, sailboarding, rowing, canoeing, and speedboating. In fact, almost any kind of boat is permitted as long as it's at least eight feet long (which leaves out plastic rafts and inflatable dinghies).

Fishing for catfish, crappie, bass, bluegills, and sunfish is also important. The California Department of Fish and Game stocks rainbow trout in winter, when the water is cooler.

You can hike in the hills, a pleasant activity in late winter, spring, and fall, when temperatures are mild. Summers can be very hot, making hiking an endurance test. A trail map at the ranger headquarters lists ten walks, none over two miles.

If you're looking for half- and full-day hikes in a cooler location, the Santa Lucia Wilderness in Los Padres National Forest is directly north of Lopez Lake, while the Garcia and Machesne Mountain Wildernesses are northeast. All three have mountain hiking trails.

Lopez Lake has one campground on the southeast shore near the entrance, with 354 tent and RV sites, a marina, a boat launch, a bait and tackle shop, and a store.

Where: Eleven miles northeast of Arroyo Grande on the west side of the coastal range, in San Luis Obispo County.
Hours: Daylight.
Admission: $4 for daytime use, $3.50 per boat. Campsites, ranging from primitive to full hookups, are $12 to $18.
Best time to visit: Year-round. Winters can be chilly; summers are very hot.
Activities: Water sports, fishing, camping, hiking.
Concessions: Campground reservations can be made six months ahead: call 805-489-8019.
Pets: Allowed on leashes.
For more information:
   Lopez Lake Recreation Area, 805-489-2095.

LAKE NACIMIENTO

Lake Nacimiento, in tree-covered lowland hills on the inland (east) side of the Santa Lucia Mountains, is a busy, multiuse, man-made lake, whose crooked fingers reach into foothill canyons along 165 miles of shoreline, creating dozens of hidden coves.

On a map, eighteen-mile-long Nacimiento looks as though it's right next to Lake San Antonio, in Monterey County to the north, but the two are twelve miles apart, occupy separate valleys divided by a high ridge, and flow into a different drainages.

Both lakes were built not for drinking water, but for flood control and irrigation; thus the water level varies as much as fifty feet. All of the land bordering the lake is private, divided among vacation homes with private docks and beaches, ranch grazing land, and some county parcels. Boaters shouldn't tie up at private docks or wherever "Private" signs are posted, but may anchor and land in undeveloped areas.

In summer, Lake Nacimiento is tremendously popular with local residents for fishing, waterskiing, and even scuba diving. The water temperatures are mild (in comparison with the ocean's 50-degree water), and the surface is calm and smooth. Since the lake isn't a source of drinking water, swimming—a great treat in this hot inland valley—is allowed. Windsurfing is allowed, but mild, variable breezes make it best for beginners.

Fishing for crappie, bass, bluegills, and trout, which are stocked regularly, is a big sport. Some of the lake's out-of-the-way fingers are the best places to hook the big ones.

Access to the lake is at Nacimiento Shores, a private resort near the dam, where boat launches, slips, fuel, and dry storage facilities are located. Daytime use fees are high ($13.50 per day), but it's a seller's market. Canoes, rowboats, and motorboat rentals are available; you'll also find bait and tackle shops, markets, and marine-supply stores. The campground has 240 tent and RV sites.

Where: On County G19, off US 101, ten miles southwest of Bradley and twenty-five miles north of Paso Robles, in San Luis Obispo County.
Hours: Daytime, except for overnight camping.
Admission: $13.50 boat-use permit and county-lake fee. Campsites range from $20 to $25 per night; $2 less for seniors.
Best time to visit: May through October.
Activities: Water sports and camping.
Concessions: Marina, slips, launch ramps, boat rentals, supplies, groceries, bait and tackle, snack bar and restaurant.

Pets: Allowed on leashes.
For more information:

Lake Nacimiento Resort, Star Route, Box 2770, Bradley CA 93426; 805-238-3256.

CARRIZO PLAIN NATURAL AREA

If earthquake activity intrigues you and the Carrizo Plain Natural Area is on the way to your destination, consider a detour through this level land, bordered by hills and marked by dry creek beds. Beneath the plain lies the infamous San Andreas Fault, running southeast between the coastal and Temblor ranges, and leaving subtle but certain evidence of immense geological forces deep in the earth.

Look for one of the most obvious signs: mismatched stream beds, where slippage along the fracture zone pushed one side past another.

Carrizo Plain, about forty-five miles long and ten miles wide, is managed by the Bureau of Land Management and the California Department of Fish and Game to protect several endangered plants and animals, including the San Joaquin kit fox, the blunt-nosed leopard lizard, the horned lark, and the sand hill crane, which winters at Soda Lake.

In addition to the animals and birds, a few hardy souls live here, too, atop the fault in California Valley, a village that was once a prosperous ranch town.

The Bureau of Land Management leads free guided caravan tours once a month on Saturday, between September and March, from 9:00 A.M. to about 3:00 P.M. If you're here at any other time, you can visit the area's two main attractions on your own.

Painted Rock, elevation 2,223 feet, sticks up from the plain off Soda Lake Road south of town. Ask for directions to this 120-foot-high sandstone hulk decorated with Native American pictographs estimated to be up to 1000 years old. Unfortunately, vandals have damaged many of the paintings, which are believed to be the work of the Chumash and Yokut peoples.

On the way back to town, stop at Soda Lake Overlook, a typical dry lake refilled annually by winter rains, providing vital seasonal wetlands for migrating birds.

Where: East of San Luis Obispo and west of the Buttonwillow exit on I-5. State 58 is the closest highway.

Hours: No limit.

Admission: No fees.

Best time to visit: Fall through spring, when wildflowers bloom. Summer is intensely hot.

Activities: Geology walks, driving tours, photography, bird-watching in spring.

Concessions: Stores in California Valley.

Pets: Allowed.

For more information:

Bureau of Land Management, 805-391-6000.

4

San Diego Area

The people who live in San Diego County say they have the world's finest climate, a claim just begging to be challenged. But once you've walked along the beach at Torrey Pines State Park at sunset, or hiked in midsummer beneath the ponderosa pines in the Santa Ana Mountains – and realized you can do it on a moment's whim, any day, year-round – you begin to understand why people rhapsodize about the place.

In the southwest corner of California, San Diego County is warmed by a constant sun and cooled by offshore breezes. The light is gold and palpable, and the days are mild. When the rains do come, usually between January and April, they bring new life, turning brown hills green overnight and renewing dry stream beds and reservoirs.

The peninsular mountains, a north-south range, divide San Diego County into coastal regions and inland valleys. Rain from the Pacific falls on the western slopes, nourishing chaparral at lower elevations and pine forests higher up. On the eastern slopes the climate is drier, giving way to the desert environment of the Salton Sea and Anza-Borrego State Park.

The peninsular mountains here are lower and rounder than the transverse ranges of Los Angeles County, and a network of roads and hiking trails makes access to most areas easy. Thus a variety of recreational uses have developed, ranging from car camping and horseback riding to backpacking along the Pacific Crest Trail, which begins at the Mexican border. Other outdoor activities include hiking, bird-watching, hunting, horseback riding, fishing, and family picnicking.

The coastal areas vary, from steep cliffs and picturesque rocky bays to sand beaches. Many private homes have been built along the coast, but there's regular access via public paths between the street or road and the beach. To find these walkways, drive as close as you can to the beach and look for signs or open channels.

Activities: Any exploration of San Diego County should begin with a good set of maps. We recommend stuffing your glove box with a combination that includes a road map, a AAA (American Automobile Association) county map, and a Cleveland National Forest map, available at National Forest district offices. If you're really into hiking, backpacking or mountain biking, add a U.S. Geological Survey topographical map.

For more information:

San Diego Convention and Visitors Bureau, 401 B Street, Suite 1400, San Diego, CA 92101; 619-232-3101.

CLEVELAND NATIONAL FOREST

The 420,630-acre Cleveland National Forest, with woods, peaks, canyons, and meadows, runs in a southeast direction from the middle of Orange and Riverside Counties to the Mexican border, a ragged ribbon of wilderness superimposed on the peninsular ranges. Cleveland is the United States' southernmost national forest.

But the forest's most prominent and surprising characteristic is the diversity of land ownership that has evolved over time. A veritable crossword puzzle of colors and textures, this national forest is spread over scattered sections owned and managed by different agencies and grouped into three administrative regions: the Trabuco, Descanso, and Palomar Ranger Districts.

To understand the pattern, look at a Forest Service map, published by the U.S. Department of Agriculture and sold at district offices. It's an invaluable tool for deciding where to hike and where to drive, and how to avoid trespassing on private holdings.

For there are many: in addition to Cleveland National Forest land, the boundaries enclose state and county parks, BLM (Bureau of Land Management) holdings, recreation areas owned and operated by private companies, private ranches, homes, vacation cottages, and towns.

There are also sixteen large and small Native American reservations, where uninvited guests aren't welcome: Pala, La Jolla, Rincon, Santa Ysabel, Pechanga, Los Coyotes, San Pasqual, Barona, Capitan Grande, Inaja, Viejas, Sycuan, Cuyapaipe, Manzanita, LaPosta, and Campo.

The Native American residents of these communities are often lumped together as Dieguenos, but culturally they belong to four different groups: the Diegueno, Cahuilla, Cupeno, and Luiseno peoples. Their ancestors were San Diego's first residents, hunting and gathering acorns in the cool canyons in summer, and moving down to the coast in winter.

After 1769, all that changed. As settlers arrived from Mexico and later the eastern United States, they carved the land into huge ranches and logged timber. In 1869, gold was discovered near the town of Julian, now a restored Western-style village and recreation area. Miners poured into the area, and further prospecting in the Santa Ana Mountains' western canyons revealed valuable deposits of zinc, lead, and silver. Finally, in 1908, the national forest was created, primarily to protect the watershed that provided water for the coast.

Four wilderness areas—San Mateo Canyon, Agua Tibia, Pine Creek, and Hauser—are the most isolated regions here. Wilderness areas, by definition, should be free of roads, but you'll occasionally find tire tracks winding through the forest, a relic of the early days. Wherever old roads remain, they're being allowed to grow over and return to their natural state.

Also within forest boundaries are Palomar Mountain State Park and Laguna Mountain Recreation Area, in the Laguna Mountains. The latter is a popular vacation destination, where developed campgrounds, stores, privately owned resorts, rental cabins, and hiking trails are clustered together.

The highest elevation in the forest, in the Laguna Mountains, is only 6,271 feet. Nonetheless, the terrain and vegetation vary greatly over the range. The western slopes, watered by Pacific clouds and storms, are greener and wetter. Snow falls occasionally in winter, accumulating in canyons and on north-facing slopes and lasting long enough for sledding, tubing, and cross-country skiing.

Chaparral typically grows at lower elevations, but above 4,000 feet, the forests shift to pine and fir. On the east side, by contrast, the mountain slopes are very arid.

Where: Cleveland National Forest runs parallel to the coastline from just below the Los Angeles County line, through Orange and Riverside Counties, to the southern border of San Diego County.
Hours: Daily, year-round.
Admission: No fee to enter Cleveland National Forest. Campground fees range from $6 to $16 per vehicle, depending on season and jurisdiction.

Best time to visit: Most areas are accessible all year, although summer and fall are sunnier and warmer.

Activities: Hiking trails, lakes for fishing, twenty-three campgrounds with 500 sites, picnic grounds. The southern end of the Pacific Crest trail begins here, near the Mexican border. Camping is allowed anywhere on national-forest land, except in Laguna Recreation Area, where you must be in a campground. Parklands under nonfederal management impose different rules.

Concessions: Supplies, gas, and groceries are available on private holdings.

Pets: Allowed on trails on leashes; not allowed within wilderness areas.

For more information:

National Forest Headquarters, 10845 Rancho Bernardo Road, San Diego, CA 92127; 619-673-6180.

Trabuco Ranger District, 1147 East Sixth Street, Corona, CA 91719; 909-736-1811.

Palomar Ranger District, 1634 Black Canyon Road, Ramona, CA 92065; 619-788-0250.

Descanso Ranger District, 3348 Alpine Boulevard., Alpine, CA 91901; 619-445-6235.

Trabuco Ranger District: The Trabuco District, in the north end of the forest, is the most unified region, with few inholdings. Within its boundaries is the San Mateo Canyon Wilderness — 39,500 roadless acres of valleys, steep canyons, and seasonal streams.

Many hikes in this district begin at trailheads in San Juan Canyon, off State 74 northeast of San Juan Capistrano. The Bear Canyon Loop Trail, 6.5 miles round-trip, which starts at Upper San Juan Campground, is a "sampler" of this wilderness, crossing through oak woodlands, up narrow canyons and over level meadows, with wildflowers, birds, and unusual rock formations.

Just south of the wilderness area and sharing its border is Camp Pendleton Marine Corps Base, off limits to recreation except with permission. (In the past, the marines have been generous in letting Boy Scout troops camp out in certain remote areas.)

At the north end of the forest (outside the wilderness area), a network of dirt roads and hiking trails can be reached from Joseph Canyon, south of Corona. Seasonal streams and creeks are found in almost every little canyon; they're most beautiful in late winter and spring when they're full of water and wildflowers are blooming everywhere. You can camp anywhere, but you need a wilderness permit.

Palomar Ranger District: This central portion of Cleveland National Forest, shaped like a hatchet, is northeast of Escondido and bisected by State 76, which runs east and west. Palomar Mountain State Park adjoins the forest near the upper east side. (For details, see the next major section.)

In the northwest corner, the 16,000-acre Agua Tibia Wilderness includes an isolated area of lowland oak forests, chaparral vegetation on the lower slopes, and pine and fir near the summit.

To hike into Agua Tibia, drive to the trailhead at Dripping Springs Campground, at 1,600 feet off State 79. Starting here, the trail forms a large loop. To reach the highest point in the wilderness area, 5,007-foot Eagle Crag Peak, hike from the trailhead 6.8 miles to the Agua Tibia Crest and from the crest another 5.5 miles south to Eagle Crag. Watch for signs marking the borders of a half-dozen Native American reservations around the perimeter of the wilderness.

Summers are very hot and water is scarce or nonexistent on most trails, so bring your own supplies. You can pick up a map and a hike description at the Palomar Ranger District office in Ramona.

Descanso Ranger District: The Descanso District, the most southerly of the three, is bisected by I-8, which crosses it from east to west and makes getting here a snap.

For a day drive through the area, pick up the Sunrise National Scenic Byway (County 1) where it begins at the intersection of State 79 south of Julian; follow it southeast along the Laguna Mountains to Laguna Mountain Recreation Area, and then loop back west and south to I-8. The route passes old-timey log cabins, crosses a historic stagecoach route and the Pacific Crest Trail, and swings out at vista points for panoramic views of the Anza-Borrego Desert to the east.

Eight-thousand-acre Laguna Mountain Recreation Area, a separate unit within Cleveland National Forest, is a multiuse outdoor vacation area for campers and hikers. A dozen well-marked trails begin in this vicinity.

Laguna Campground has 103 developed tent and RV sites, available by reservation or on a first-come first-served basis. Laguna Lodge has rental cabins and a small grocery and supply store. The area's one restaurant, the Sunrise Café, serves home-cooked food.

Two small ponds sport the grand titles of Big Laguna Lake and Little Laguna Lake; there's no swimming or fishing in either one, but they're picturesque in spring when the water level is high and the wildflowers are in bloom.

Also in this district are two wilderness areas, both south of I-8. The 13,100-acre Pine Creek Wilderness can be reached from either of two trailheads: Horsethief Trailhead, on the west border off Japatul Lyons Valley Road, or Pine Creek Trailhead, near Pine Valley just north of I-8. The wilderness is somewhat isolated, and wildlife thrives. Keep an eye peeled for deer, coyotes, gray foxes, mountain lions, bobcats, lizards, snakes, ground squirrels, and numerous hawks and owls.

The 8,000-acre Hauser Wilderness, to the south, is semi-arid and stark, devoid of trails except in the lower southeast, where the Pacific Crest Trail crosses the corner. The mountains'

Mountain lion

slopes are rocky and steep, with a mixture of chaparral and desert vegetation. Practically on the Mexican border, the Hauser Wilderness is hot and dry and, unless you're a student of semi-arid habitats, inhospitable.

Where: In Cleveland National Forest.

Hours: No limit.

Admission: No fees for daytime use. National Forest Campground fees vary from $6 to $16 per vehicle per night.

Best time to visit: Forested areas in the north are nice year-round. Exposed chaparral slopes are very hot and dry in summer.

Activities: Hiking, camping, bird-watching, scenic drives. Chains are required when driving in the mountains in winter.

Concessions: Laguna Lodge, 619-473-8533, and Sunrise Café.

Pets: Allowed on leashes.

For more information:

Trabuco Ranger District, 1147 East Sixth Street, Corona, CA 91719; 909-736-1811.

Palomar Ranger District, 1634 Black Canyon Road, Ramona, CA 92065; 619-788-0250.

Descanso Ranger District, 3348 Alpine Boulevard, Alpine, CA 91901; 619-445-6235.

PALOMAR MOUNTAIN STATE PARK AND MOUNT PALOMAR OBSERVATORY

One of our annual easy-camping weekends is in Observatory Campground below the summit of 6,100-foot Mount Palomar, on the border of 1,897-acre Palomar Mountain State Park, where a 2.5-mile trail winds through tall pines, heading for the summit and the world-famous Hale telescope.

Though space-age technology has created new ways of exploring the heavens, the telescope, which was installed here on Palomar Mountain in 1947, is still the world's largest working single-lens telescope. Every night when the sky is clear and dark, the gleaming white dome slides open and astronomers pursue their work, charting the skies and plumbing the mysteries of deep space.

The telescope's achievements have been many, and they've far surpassed its humble beginnings. In 1934, the Corning Glass Works in Corning, New York—yes, the same folks who brought you oven cookware—poured the 200-inch mirror of Pyrex glass. For eight months the twenty-ton disk sat and cooled; then it was boxed and shipped to Pasadena.

The grinding and polishing of the glass began immediately, as did the construction of the observatory. By 1947, the mirror, shaped to a slim 14.5 tons and backed with a paper-thin layer of aluminum, was ready to be installed.

To see the telescope and the observatory and tour the small museum, open daily to the public, drive to the end of County S6, park, and look for the entrance. To stargaze, choose a moonless night and bring sleeping bags or blankets; even in summer the evenings are chilly.

Hiking trails in Cleveland National Forest wind through thick forests of Coulter and Jeffrey pine, white fir, incense cedar, and grassy meadows. One of the trails goes to the observatory from Observatory Campground, one of four in the vicinity. Observatory and Fry Creek Campgrounds, both in the national forest, are available on a first-come first-served basis. Reservations are accepted at Palomar Mountain State Park Campground and the county-park campground. Anglers can cast into Doane Lake, a small pond stocked with trout. The lake is named for George Doane, who homesteaded the area in the 1880s and planted apple orchards.

Where: Northeast of San Diego, off County S7, via County S6 and State 76.

Hours: The observatory is open daily between 9:00 A.M. and 4:30 P.M.

Admission: No admission fee to the observatory or state park. Campground fees vary from $6 to $16 per vehicle per night.

Best time to visit: Summer, fall, and early winter. Late winter and spring are often foggy.

Activities: Tour the observatory, see the telescope, and visit the museum, where exhibits detail the telescope's history and achievements. Camping reservations should be made through MISTIX (800-444-7275), or on a first-come first-served basis.
Concessions: None in the park. Some small markets and rustic cafés located in private sections nearby.
Pets: Allowed on leashes.
For more information:
Palomar Observatory, 35899 Canfield Road, Palomar Mountain, San Diego, CA 92128; 619-742-2119.
Palomar Mountain State Park, 619-765-0755.

CUYAMACA RANCHO STATE PARK

Cuyamaca Rancho State Park, one of San Diego County's less widely known parks, is also one of the most scenic. The 24,677-acre park, on the crest of the Laguna Mountains, with elevations ranging from 3,400 to 6,512 feet, is on the east border of Cleveland National Forest's Descanso District, about forty miles northeast of San Diego.

The Anza-Borrego Desert is directly east, but Cuyamaca's upper mountain slopes, especially on the Pacific side, are forested and green, watered by clouds and moisture from the ocean. Summers are very warm; winters are chilly, with occasional snow dusting the mountaintops, but melting quickly.

Since few people know about Cuyamaca Rancho, trails and campgrounds are quiet and uncrowded, except on holiday weekends. Hiking trails and dirt fire roads cross the backcountry, winding through open meadows, oak forests, and pine forests on the upper mountain elevations and along seasonal creeks. Three hundred bird species have been identified.

Cuyamaca Rancho made newspaper headlines in 1992, after several mountain-lion attacks on children camping with their parents. The attacks occurred during a drought, when the animals were under stress and short of food; rangers subsequently tracked and killed the lion, but the incidents created unnecessary panic. Normally mountain lions are seldom seen and rarely bother people.

State 79 bisects the park, running north and south near the crest. To the west of the highway, the terrain is wooded; to the east it's chaparral. Some of the 100 miles of dirt roads and hiking trails start from points near the road. All are open to hikers, mountain bikers, and horseback riders, but not to private cars.

A favorite "peak-bagger's" hike is the four-mile trail to the summit of Cuyamaca Peak, the park's highest point. The trail, moderately steep, climbs 1,592 feet from Pasa Picacho Campground, heading west and south toward the summit. The view from the top is worth the effort; on a clear day you can see the Pacific Ocean, the Colorado Desert in Anza-Borrego State Park, the Salton Sea, and even Mexico. Another, easier hike from the same campground is the climb up 5,730-foot Stonewall Peak, a two-mile hike to the east, with only 860 feet of elevation gain.

The state-park headquarters are along the north border, on State 79. The visitors center has interpretive nature exhibits and displays on the Native American inhabitants and regional mining.

Where: The southern border is nine miles north of I-8, on State 79. Or take State 78 from Escondido and turn south on State 79.
Hours: Daytime use or overnight camping. Campground gates are open 8:00 A.M. to 10:00 P.M. With reservations, check into the campsite between 2:00 P.M. and 10:00 P.M. After hours, automatic check-in with the "Iron Ranger," an electronic gate-entry system.
Admission: No admission fee for daytime use. Campsites are $14 to $16 per vehicle per night.
Best time to visit: May through October.

Activities: Camping, hiking, bird-watching, horseback riding, picnicking.
Concessions: The visitors center has exhibits. There are two campgrounds for tents and RVs, two for group camping, and two for horse camping.
Pets: Dogs allowed on leashes; $1 extra per day.
For more information:
    Cuyamaca Rancho State Park, 619-765-0755.

LAKE SKINNER COUNTY PARK

Fishermen pull record-setting striped bass out of Lake Skinner County Park, northeast of Temecula in Riverside County. The biggest striper ever, landed in the month of October, weighed in at 39.8 pounds, and twenty-pounders aren't unusual.

But the 6,440-acre park, in semiarid rolling hills, is also in demand for camping, especially in spring and fall when the climate is mild. Between July and September, midday temperatures typically push 100 degrees or more, and it helps to be a sun worshipper if you're planning on boating for any length of time.

The lake, with 1,200 surface acres and twelve miles of shoreline, is a man-made reservoir for drinking water, so body-contact sports aren't allowed. Small boats, rafts, and canoes, which would interfere with motorboats, aren't permitted.

Local wildlife agencies stock the lake with rainbow trout twice a month between November and May, when the water is cool. Striped bass, largemouth bass, bluegills, crappie, and catfish flourish on their own year-round.

The campground has 257 sites, some shaded by sycamore and eucalyptus trees planted for the purpose. Reservations aren't required, but are advised for all weekends and holidays. A swimming pool is open from June through September, a bonus for families with children.

Where: Eight miles northeast of Temecula, near State 79.

Hours: Daylight hours or overnight camping.

Admission: $4 for daytime use. Campsites are $12 per night for cars, $17 for RVs with full hookups. Make reservations through MISTIX (800-444-7275).

Best time to visit: Year-round.

Activities: Camping and fishing.

Concessions: Marina store, 909-926-1505.

Pets: Allowed on leashes.

For more information:

Lake Skinner County Park Headquarters, 909-926-1541.

Marina, 909-926-1505.

SAN PASQUAL BATTLEFIELD STATE HISTORIC PARK

As you drive through bucolic San Pasqual Valley on a sunny day, with the distant hills etched gray-green on the horizon and golden meadows and irrigated farm fields in the foreground, it's hard to imagine the foggy December dawn when a troop of Mexican cavalry trounced a band of American soldiers on this battlefield.

The year was 1846, and the Mexican War was simmering. American troops led by Stephen Kearny and guided by Kit Carson were marching to San Diego when they stumbled onto Gen. Andres Pico and a band of eighty riders.

The Mexicans, skilled horsemen wielding razor-sharp lances with deadly accuracy, struck and struck again, killing twenty-two Americans and wounding many more before fading into the mist. The Mexicans had proved their mettle, but the tide of history and geography was against them. A month later, the Mexicans were defeated, and California became an American state a few years later.

There are no relics to be found at San Pasqual Battlefield State Historic Park. A single stone monument commemorates the bravery of the Mexicans and the determination of the Americans. The hills are still, and your imagination must paint the scene as it once was.

But exhibits and a slide show in the small visitors center recapture the sights and sounds of that long-ago day, when the clash of metal, the thunder of hooves, and the shouts of victory filled the valley.

Where: Seven miles east of Escondido on State 78, just past the entrance to the San Diego Wild Animal Park.

Hours: Open daily.

Admission: Free.

Best time to visit: Year-round, or in conjunction with a trip to the San Diego Wild Animal Park.

Activities: View the battlefield and tour the museum.

Pets: Allowed on leashes inside; not allowed in visitors center.

Concessions: None.

For more information:

San Pasqual Battlefield State Historic Park, 15808 San Pasqual Valley Road, Escondido, CA 92027; 619-489-0076.

SAN DIEGO WILD ANIMAL PARK

The fields of grazing giraffes and white-bearded gnus look like Kenya, but are actually in San Diego County. The hot sun and grassy hills feel like the veldt, but are instead San Pasqual Valley, surrounded by low mountains. This is the San Diego Wild Animal Park, an adjunct of the San Diego Zoo, founded in 1970 and dedicated to the study, protection, and breeding of threatened and endangered animal species.

More than 250 species at risk live at the park, with 2,500 individual animals running free in natural outdoor enclosures, each representing a different world area: East Africa, South Africa, Asian Plains, Asian Waterhole, and Australia.

Compatible animals with similar habits and from the same world region are grouped together. Predators and animals difficult to manage—elephants and tigers, for instance—have their own enclosures. Tall, camouflaged fences—called "inrigging," with overhanging tops nearly invisible to people, but seen easily by the animals—separate the enclosures. There are no lions at the park because they're not, as yet, on the threatened-species list.

At the San Diego Wild Animal Park,
visitors are confined and the animals run free

Though public entertainment wasn't part of the park's original purpose, zoo officials realized quickly that the public's support and involvement were essential to make the project self-supporting. Thus it was designed to please and inform as well as to protect. Since opening day, in 1972, conservation education has been an ever-growing part of the mission.

There are several ways to see the park. If you plan to spend the day here, we suggest trying them all. Start with a fifty-minute guided tour on the Wgasa Bush Line, an open-air monorail built on the hills above the park. The narrated ride, which circles the park, gives you an overview of the layout and a panoramic view of the animal herds.

Your guide stops at various points of interest and fills in with an assortment of facts. Flamingos won't reproduce unless there are at least 100 birds in a flock; California condors breed just fine if you leave them alone and give them room; the golden eagles circling overhead are volunteers, freeloaders getting fat on the gophers that snitch animal feed.

After the ride, walk around the 1.75-mile Kilimanjaro Trail for a closer look at some of the smaller exhibits: the Sumatran tiger's woody hollow, the two-acre African elephant habitat, the maned-wolf enclosure, and the cheetah's grassy plain. From Pumzika Point there's a wide-angle view of the East Africa enclosure.

If you're here in the summer, plan to join a "photo caravan" for groups of five to ten people—minisafaris in an open truck driving into the enclosures on dirt roads. The short safari (1.5 hours) visits two enclosures; the long safari (3.5 hours) visits four.

The guides stop the truck at intervals for picture taking and to hand out apples and carrots for you to feed to the rhinos and giraffes. The caravans fill up fast, and advance reservations are suggested.

Finally, attend a bird or elephant show, join a behind-the-scenes tour, shop at one of the gift stores, or eat lunch at one of several outdoor cafés – or all of the above. During the summer, music concerts are held in the amphitheater near the park on weekend evenings.

Where: Thirty miles northwest of San Diego on State 78.

Hours: Daily 9:00 A.M. to 5:00 P.M. between mid-June and Labor Day; to 4:00 P.M. the rest of the year.

Admission: $17.45 for ages twelve and up, $10.45 for ages three to eleven, $15.70 for seniors. Parking is $2 per vehicle.

Best time to visit: April, the calving season, is exciting. Spring, fall, and winter are pleasant. Summer is very hot and busy.

Activities: Wildlife caravans tour the large animal exhibits daily in summer and irregularly in winter. You must have reservations to be assured of a place. Guided monorail rides around the park run continuously. Animal handlers give demonstrations and talks at the small-animal exhibits.

Concessions: Snack bars and outdoor cafés serve food. Shops sell gifts, souvenirs, animal books, posters, t-shirts, and postcards.

Pets: Not allowed.

For more information:

San Diego Wild Animal Park, 15500 San Pasqual Valley Road, Escondido, CA 92027; 619-747-8702.

SAN DIEGO COUNTY STATE BEACHES

The San Diego coast is dotted with city and county beaches, but most are very small and open only for daytime use. Two state beaches, San Clemente, on the Orange–San Diego County line, and San Onofre, have campground facilities.

San Clemente State Beach and **San Onofre State Beach**, both favorites with surf fishermen, are beach parks with high cliffs above the ocean and secluded beaches below, accessible from trails that climb down the bluffs. The tops of the bluffs, where the campsites are located, are good vantage points for whale watching between November and March. Swimming in small pods, the migrating whales pass this point on their way to and from Baja California.

San Clemente State Beach, on 110 acres, has 157 campsites, seventy-two of them with RV hookups; the north end of the beach is reserved for surfing. If you're traveling north or south, this is a good park for a pleasant overnight stay.

San Onofre, three miles farther south, is both larger and wilder, with 3,036 acres, 3.5 miles of shoreline, and a half-dozen trails cut into the sandstone cliffs. The beach at the base of the cliffs is partly sand and good for swimming, and partly marshy wetlands around the inlet where San Mateo Creek flows into the ocean. Trestles Beach, a famous surfing spot, is also here.

While the beach below is primitive and unspoiled, from the top of the cliffs, where 221 campsites are located, you can see the white towers of the San Onofre Nuclear Reactors — an unsettling experience perhaps.

Where: San Clemente State Beach is off I-5 at San Clemente; San Onofre is off I-5 three miles south of San Clemente.
Hours: Open daily.
Admission: Free for daytime use; fees for camping and parking.
Best time to visit: Year-round.
Activities: Swimming, surfing, surf fishing, jogging, bird-watching.
Concessions: None.
Pets: Allowed on leashes.
For more information:
   San Clemente State Beach, 714-492-0802.
   San Onofre State Beach, 714-492-4872.

State Park Orange Coast District Headquarters, 714-492-0802.

TORREY PINES STATE RESERVE AND STATE BEACH

This wild and solitary 1,082-acre park, with sand beaches, salt marshes, and sandstone bluffs, was founded to protect a botanical dinosaur: one of the world's last two remaining Torrey pine forests. The other is far away on Santa Rosa Island, in California Channel Islands National Park.

The pines, numbering about 6,000, were widespread during the last Ice Age when the climate was cold. As the climate warmed gradually, their range began to shrink. Under natural conditions the trees reproduce slowly, but they've also been threatened by squirrels, which eat the seeds, and by cycles of drought. Normally, mature specimens are straight and tall, but here on the coast, buffeted by offshore winds, they're gnarled and weathered.

While the trees are interesting relics, Los Penasquitos Marsh, along the coast, plays a more significant role as a protected habitat for resident and migratory birds. The loss of brackish marshes and inland wetlands threatens migratory birds, which are finding fewer and fewer places to land, feed, and rest during their long trek north and south.

In Los Penasquitos you may see snowy egrets, mallards, pintails, grebes, great blue herons, and loons. The sandstone cliffs above the beach, a mottled coffee-and-cream color, were formed twenty million years ago. Look for fossils wherever layers of stone are exposed. Nature trails wind through the trees and along the bluffs. The visitors center, in an old pueblo-style adobe house, has nature exhibits and books.

Where: Entrance on County S21, south of Del Mar.
Hours: Daytime use only. The visitors center is open daily.

Admission: Free for foot traffic. $4 per car on weekends, $3 on weekdays.

Best time to visit: Spring through fall.

Activities: Swimming, surf fishing, hiking, picnicking.

Concessions: Visitors center. No food. Parking is limited.

Pets: Allowed on leashes; not allowed on trails.

For more information:

   Torrey Pines State Reserve and State Beach, 619-755-2063.

5

The Deserts

More than one newcomer to California's twenty-five million acres of desert land has been startled to find not tall dunes of shifting sand, but miles of shrubs, trees, wildflowers, narrow canyons, rocky peaks, dry lakes, granite mounts, and weathered pinnacles.

Big dunes do exist in a few places here, but they're a small part of a much greater whole. Indeed, for the wayfarer who takes time to pause, listen, and explore, there are immense beauty, considerable diversity, and abundant life in these remarkable arid lands.

MOJAVE DESERT

The Mojave Desert lies to the north and east of the San Gabriel and San Bernardino Mountains and extends east into Nevada. Known locally as "the high desert," with elevations above 3,000 feet, the Mojave's summers are hot and dry and its winters cold, punctuated by torrential rainstorms and an occasional snowfall.

"The low desert," the Colorado Desert (a subarea of the Sonoran Desert), lies to the south, from Joshua Tree National Monument south toward the Mexican border and east toward Arizona. Elevations in the low desert are generally below 3000 feet, temperatures are warmer year-round, and winters are pleasant, as anyone who's wintered in Palm Springs will attest.

The Anza-Borrego Desert, east of San Diego, is also considered part of the Colorado Desert, although some of the mountain peaks rimming the north and west boundaries are higher than 6,000 feet.

History: In the early days of Western settlement, most explorers and the pioneers that followed them regarded the deserts as wasteland – barren and dangerous regions to be crossed quickly and as soon forgotten.

Even after 1910, when the automobile made cross-country travel easier, visitors to Southern California treated a desert crossing with respect. After reaching the Mojave's east border, they stopped to wait for nightfall, napping in the shade or renting a room for a few hours' sleep. As the sun set, they resumed the journey, driving all night to reach the coast before dawn.

Today, with the best coastal land gone, developers are looking to desert lands with new eyes – particularly the western Mojave, within commuting distance of Los Angeles. Tract housing has sprouted on dry hills, and irrigation has replaced sage and creosote bushes with grass. The herds of thousands of pronghorn antelope that once roamed Antelope Valley were gone by 1913, and the vast fields of California poppies, the state flower, have shrunk in size.

Proposed Mojave National Park: The East Mojave Desert, a vast territory stretching north and east into Nevada, is still isolated and wild. In 1981, the federal government designated 1.5 million acres in the eastern Mojave, ninety percent of it already owned by state and federal agencies, as the East Mojave National Scenic Area in recognition of its unique resources. Soon after, legislation was introduced in the U.S. Congress to convert the area to a new park, Mojave National Park.

The bill is currently in Congress, but stalled by an amendment to exempt from protection Lanfair Valley, a 290,000-acre region in the heart of the proposed park containing some of the most significant geological sites.

Ironically, opposition to the bill comes not from the eight property owners who live in Lanfair Valley, but from a group of lobbyists and congressmen who have never been to the East Mojave Desert, but who routinely block all parkland bills on behalf of anticonservation interests.

Be prepared: Despite increased visitor use, many of California's deserts are still very remote. Always carry extra water, food, warm clothes, tools for minor car repairs, and, in some areas, extra gasoline. If your car breaks down, stay with the vehicle and signal for help. A CB radio could be a lifesaver. After rain or thunderstorms, watch for flash flooding.

Best time to visit: Spring and fall, then winter.
Activities: Nature observation, bird-watching, hiking, camping, photography, car trips.
Concessions: Uncertain. Always bring your own water, food, clothes, and supplies. A CB radio doesn't hurt, either.
Pets: Keep them on leashes. Rattlesnakes and cactus spines present hazards to domestic animals.
For more information: Road maps, county maps, and U.S. Geological Survey topographical maps provide a wealth of detail to make your trip more interesting and easier to plan.

WEST MOJAVE DESERT

The western half of the Mojave Desert, close to Los Angeles, is more developed. It's also more convenient for day trips. The

Beep, beep: roadrunner...

following parks and preserves have been established to provide recreation and to protect vanishing desert habitats.

Devil's Punchbowl County Park

Among the mighty works of nature, "earthquake" is a dirty word, especially in Los Angeles. But not at the Devil's Punchbowl, twenty-four miles southeast of Palmdale on the southern edge of the Mojave Desert. Here in this 1,310-acre county park, earthquake power has forged a geologic marvel, a deep chasm filled with jumbled and tilted sandstone slabs and spires.

The problem with earthquakes, at least for the geologists who study them, is that the shakes and rattles are over almost as soon as they've begun. But at the Punchbowl, elevation 4,700 feet, where the desert floor rises to meet the San Gabriel Mountains, the San Andreas, Pinyon, and Punchbowl faults converge in a one- to two-mile-wide fracture zone deep below the crust.

As constant movement along the faults slides the Mojave Desert past the mountains, moving at a rate of two inches per year, relentless pressure forces the underlying sandstone layers upward. Over the millennia, erosion by wind and water has worn away the softer rock, scooping out a bowl-shaped depression and molding the harder sandstone pinnacles.

Several hiking trails begin at the park or loop around it. The most traveled is the one-mile Loop Nature Trail that descends 300 feet among tall boulders to the canyon floor, through a juniper and pinyon-pine forest and a specialized high-desert wildlife community. The trail follows Punchbowl Creek, full of water in the spring and early summer, before climbing back to the rim.

The second most popular trail is the 3.7-mile hike to the Devil's Chair, a narrow, chalk-white finger of rock projecting over the canyon floor. The trail circles behind the Punchbowl on the side of the mountains, through digger- and ponderosa-pine forests, before dropping down to the Chair. From this point, the trail, also open to horseback riders and mountain bikers, continues on to South Fork Campground, where it connects to other Angeles National Forest trails.

Rock climbers practice maneuvers on some of the steeper sandstone pinnacles, although park rangers are increasingly concerned over damage to the rocks from pitons and nails.

"I've always welcomed climbers," says Ranger Jack Farley, "but there are more of them now, and they're putting in more routes faster than ever, using battery-powered drills and masonry bits. They can drill a hole in a few seconds, and we can't see or hear them do it. They know the rules, but they think just one more hole won't hurt."

Although artifacts found in the area indicate that Native Americans once lived here, the Punchbowl wasn't officially discovered until 1853, during an expedition to scout railroad routes to the coast. For years afterward, the area was too isolated for general use; then in the late 1950s, Los Angeles County bought land on the rim and built a road and a parking lot. The present park was founded in 1963.

A visitors center near the rim was remodeled recently, with glass exhibit cases for animal skeletons, arrowheads, grinding bowls, mounted bird specimens, and a collection of orphaned live animals, including a Pacific rattler, a gopher snake, a tarantula, scorpions, and a gecko.

Outdoors near the rim, a "rehab" aviary for injured birds houses several great horned owls and a barn owl, all brought in after near-fatal collisions with barbed wire and city power lines. Picnickers will find tables among the pine trees near the visitors center.

Where: About seventy miles from downtown Los Angeles and twenty-four miles southeast of Palmdale. The park is on County N6, seven miles off State 138 (the Pearblossom Highway), east of Pearblossom.

Hours: Sunrise to sunset. The visitors center opens intermittently.

Admission: No fees to enter, but donations are requested. There's a $3 fee to park on weekends and holidays.

Best time to visit: Spring and fall. Winters are beautiful, but occasional heavy snow may close the trails.

Activities: Hiking, nature walks, horseback riding, geologic and animal observation, picnicking.

Concessions: Bathrooms. No food; no overnight camping.

Pets: Allowed on leashes.

For more information:
Devil's Punchbowl County Park, 805-944-2743.

Antelope Valley Poppy Preserve

For most of the year, the hills in the Antelope Valley Poppy Preserve look like all the other hills nearby — gently undulating mounds covered with dry, straw-colored grass. But each year between February and May, they're transformed into a sea of shimmering orange—the bright petals of thousands of California poppies, the state flower.

Poppies once grew in abundance over Antelope Valley and the surrounding foothills, blooming each spring for four to six weeks. As development has spread the poppies have disappeared, so in 1976, the 1,630-acre Antelope Valley Poppy Preserve was established in a particularly fertile and productive section.

In 1982 the visitors center opened, with local- and natural-history displays and a slide show on the living cycles of desert wildflowers. The visitors center is open daily during the spring bloom and on weekends the rest of the year.

You can see the poppies from your car window or walk among them on seven miles of trails varying from a half-mile to two miles long, climbing to several viewpoints near Antelope Buttes.

Bring a camera and tripod for good close-ups of the poppies, and of lupine, cream cups, coreopsis, locoweed, tidy tips and dandelions. A picnic area has tables and grills. There's no overnight camping.

Where: Fourteen miles from Lancaster, off State 14 and Lancaster Road (Avenue I).
Hours: Daylight hours.
Admission: $5 per car.
Best time to visit: February through May. If you send a self-addressed, stamped postcard to the visitors center, volunteers will mail it back the following early spring, two weeks before the flowers are expected to bloom.
Activities: Wildflower viewing, photography, nature walks, picnicking.
Concessions: Visitors center. Food and gas available in Lancaster.
Pets: Allowed on leashes.

For more information:
Antelope Valley Poppy Preserve, 805-942-0662.

SADDLEBACK BUTTE STATE PARK

It's hot in the Mojave Desert on August 12th, even at night. But the summit of Saddleback Butte, in Saddleback Butte State Park, is one of the darkest, clearest places to watch the Perseid meteor shower's annual shooting-star display.

How much longer visitors can count on dark nights and great views is another issue. Housing and towns are gobbling up the western Mojave Desert – one of the reasons this park has become so important.

The butte is a single granite mount rising 1,000 feet above the broad alluvial plain of Antelope Valley, visible from miles around. Everyone who can climbs to the 3,641-foot summit, on a moderate four-mile loop trail, for incredible panoramic views of the desert landscape.

The 2,875-acre park was established in 1960, not only to protect the butte, but to preserve a fine stand of Joshua trees, once abundant and now disappearing gradually around the base. Pronghorn antelope, for which the valley was named, were also abundant here, roving in herds over the land in search of good pasturage.

Then in 1876, the Southern Pacific Railroad laid tracks across the Mojave Desert to connect the Tehachapi Pass to Lancaster and Palmdale. Although the roadbed occupied only a narrow corridor of unfenced land, the antelope refused to cross the tracks. Deprived of their best grazing land, they died of starvation during several bad winters in the 1880s.

An estimated 70,000 people use the park each year, especially during the spring when the wildflowers bloom. A picnic area with twenty-five tables, grills, and shade ramadas adjoins the visitors center.

The campground, one mile south of the visitors center, is one of few in the desert with fresh piped water. The self-guided half-mile Joshua Nature Trail, marked with interpretive displays, starts at the visitors center. The trail to the butte begins in the same area.

The Antelope Valley Indian Museum: While you're in the area, include a visit to the Antelope Valley Indian Museum. (You may have to call and arrange it in advance.) This amazing building houses a large and unusual collection of Native American art.

The museum, formerly a house, belonged to H. Arden Edwards, a self-taught artist and homesteader. He designed it to harmonize with its rocky surroundings; with remarkable foresight, he also incorporated various energy-conservation techniques.

Three sides of the house are built inside the bedrock of Piute Butte, with huge boulders exposed in the interior, keeping the house cooler in summer and warmer in winter. The rooms, walls, and lighting were placed specifically to show off Edwards' collection of Native American art.

In the late 1930s, Edwards sold the house to Grace Oliver, an amateur anthropologist and fellow collector of Native American art. She combined the two collections, expanded the building, and opened it as a private museum in 1938. In 1979, the local museum-support group arranged for its purchase by the state.

Guided docent tours are held Tuesdays, Thursdays, and some Saturdays. Call to arrange a tour and to check opening hours.

Where: The park is nineteen miles east of Lancaster, in San Bernardino County. The entrance is on East Avenue J and 170th Street. The museum is seventeen miles east of State 14 on Avenue M, between 150th and 170th Streets East.

Hours: The park is open daylight to dusk, except for campers. The museum is open every other weekend, except from July through September (the hot months), but makes arrangements for individual visits. Call to schedule a time.

Admission: $5 per vehicle for daytime use, $10 per night to camp.

Best time to visit: Spring, during the wildflower displays.

Activities: Hiking, nature walks, camping, stargazing, kite flying.

Concessions: Visitors center. Campground with fifty sites, tables, grills (bring your own wood), flush toilets, piped water. RVs to 30 feet allowed. No reservations required.

Pets: Allowed on leashes.

For more information:
Saddleback Butte State Park, 805-942-0662.

RED ROCK CANYON STATE PARK

Some of the Mojave Desert's most spectacular rock formations are at Red Rock Canyon State Park—a desert landmark, stagecoach station, and, in recent years, a western movie set. Our first in-person look at the park's narrow canyons, steep cliffs, and strange spires was during a recent filming, when a friend in the props department asked us out to watch the goings-on.

State 14, a paved road running north and south through the 10,384-acre park, is the same historic wagon road that has connected Los Angeles with points north since the early days. Now it divides the park into two areas: Hagen Canyon Natural Preserve to the west and Red Cliffs Natural Preserve to the east.

Since graded dirt roads circle both areas, you can do some sight-seeing from your car window. But the interior of both preserves is open to foot traffic only. For the best views, walk up and into the canyons between the pinnacles. Stop at the Ricardo Ranger Station and visitors center first, just off State 14, to pick up maps of the park and ask about road conditions. An interpretive nature trail with trailside exhibits also starts from this area.

The park, located on the northern edge of the Mojave Desert, lies in a transition zone between the desert and the southern Sierra Nevadas. Some characteristics of both zones can be observed here, and the lists of identified animals and birds is more varied than is typical for the desert.

Rangers report occasional glimpses of ring-tailed cats, kangaroo rats, desert iguanas, leopard lizards, snakes, and owls. More frequently seen mammals include rabbits, kit foxes, squirrels, and bats. The list of identified birds includes hawks, owls, cactus wrens, Say's phoebes, roadrunners, horned larks, crissal

A big-eared kit fox

thrashers, shrikes, quail, and chukar. Vegetation, sparse on the exposed rocks, includes Joshua trees, creosote bushes, and desert holly in protected canyons.

The origin of these red sedimentary rocks was ten million years ago on a vast sea bottom, as countless layers of sand, silt, and marine organisms drifted slowly down and hardened. Over time, the layers were covered by two different volcanic flows, of softer and harder material. When the sedimentary rocks were finally uplifted and tilted, erosion by wind and water created their present shapes.

Where the hard lava layers resisted erosion, they became cap rocks above softer layers below. On the exposed cliffs, thousands of layers of accumulated materials record gradual temperature and climate variations over eons.

Occasionally, scientists find portions of fossil bones and teeth—the remains of mastodons, saber-toothed tigers, miniature horses, rhinos, and wolves. They serve as indicators that not too long ago—geologically speaking—the climate was milder and wetter, and that today's desert conditions are a relatively new phenomenon.

Geological and natural history aside, it's the bold look of the rocks—their surrealistic shapes and vivid colors intensified by the luminous light of the desert—that brings both sightseers and photographers to the park. Bands of color splashed on the cliffs and pinnacles—ivory, chalk, beige, tan, peach, rust, chocolate, and coffee—change in hue with the passing hours.

Here, as elsewhere in the desert, prospectors anticipated big gold strikes. One of them, Edward Hagen, bought most of the land in expectation of a bonanza and founded the small town of Ricardo, named for his son Richard. Because the rocks were easy to spot from afar, they became a landmark and stagecoach stop on the road from Los Angeles to nearby mining towns and Owens Valley.

In 1969, the state created the recreation area, permitting use by off-road vehicles (ORVs), which quickly damaged the fragile terrain. In 1980, Red Rock Canyon was transferred to the California State Parks Department, and ORVs were forbidden. Of the present total acreage, 8220 acres are administered by the state, and 2164 acres belong to the Bureau of Land Management.

Winters can be quite cold and summers very hot. In spring, wildflowers soften the landscape. The visitors center has flower-identification checklists.

Where: Twenty-five miles northeast of Mojave on State 14.
Hours: Daylight, or overnight camping.
Admission: $5 per car for daytime use. Camping is $7 per night. Reservations not required.
Best time to visit: Spring.
Activities: Camping, picnicking, hiking, desert exploration, photography, nature observation.
Concessions: The campground near the visitors center is open year-round. Fifty primitive campsites have tables, grills, piped water, and pit toilets, or you can camp anywhere nearby on BLM land. Bring your own food, firewood, and supplies. No phone at the park.
Pets: Allowed on leashes.
For more information:

Red Rock Canyon State Park, RRC Box 26, Cantil, CA 93519.

High Desert Headquarters, Gen. Wm. J. Fox Airfield, 4555 West Avenue G, Lancaster, CA 93534; 805-942-0662.

EAST MOJAVE NATIONAL SCENIC AREA

The East Mojave National Scenic Area covers 1.5 million acres, a vast and virtually untouched wilderness with few developed facilities, visitor attractions, or paved roads. You're on your own when you travel out here.

Most of the land within the boundaries has no specific park or preserve affiliation, other than its designation as Bureau of Land Management (BLM) land. The area is currently proposed for national-park status, to be named Mojave National Park. Some areas that will be within the park are described below.

As you explore, remember that some land may be owned or leased by private individuals. Unless you know for sure who owns a particular piece of property, avoid trespassing near buildings or homes or in enclosed yards. Fenced but empty land usually belongs to the BLM. Local BLM employees can tell you which lands are private and which are public. If confrontations with so-called owners arise, report them to area officials. Automobile-club maps for San Bernardino County are excellent for desert exploration.

California Desert Information Center: Though not actually within the East Mojave Scenic Area, the exhibits and displays in this visitors center, operated by the Bureau of Land Management, detail the human and natural history, geology, and wildlife of the eastern Mojave Desert. You can also get information on weather, roads, and recreation. It's located in Barstow at 831 Barstow Road, at the junction of I-15 and I-40. Call 619-256-8313.

Kelso Dunes: These are the classic dunes—thousands of acres of champagne sand heaped 600 feet high, blowing and shifting in the wind, but always staying in the same place. Actually, some sand does blow away, but it's replenished continually by new sand wafting in from the Devil's Playground to the northwest.

You can climb to the top in an hour or two. Listen for the famed "singing" noises as thin sheets of sand slide over one another. If you find yourself between two dunes with only the sky as a reference point, you may feel as though you've been beamed up to another planet.

The dunes are located north of I-40 and west of Kelbaker Road, almost due west of Providence Mountains State Recreation Area.

Cima Dome: Evidence of volcanic activity in the region, this rounded dome is a batholith—a column of molten rock that pushed up through the earth, was lifted later above the desert floor, and was finally weathered by the elements.

The Cima Dome, approximately seventy-five square miles in size and 1,500 feet tall, is so large and tree-covered (with a healthy stand of Joshua trees) that from a distance it looks like any other hill and may be tough to identify.

Trails climb to the 5,701-foot top and to the top of 5,755-foot Teutonia Peak on the dome's north slope. The dome is about twenty miles southeast of I-15, northwest of Cima, on Kelso Cima Road.

Afton Canyon: The Mojave River flows underground for most of its length, but in 600-foot-deep Afton Canyon it flows above ground throughout the year, attracting birds, animals, and an entire riparian community. The route through the canyon, which Kit Carson, Jedediah Smith, and other explorers called the Mojave Road, provided access to water, vital for long desert crossings. A campground in the canyon has twenty-two sites, piped water, tables, toilets, and grills.

Afton Canyon is just beyond the westernmost boundary of the East Mojave National Scenic Area, off I-15 and Afton Canyon Road.

New York Mountains: The New York Mountains are the highest range in the East Mojave, reaching elevations of 7,532 feet in Lanfair Valley. Because of their size, the mountains and their vegetation are very diverse, with canyons, valleys, and rocky peaks covered with desert and semidesert plants. Hiking trails into the upper canyons and slopes are used by bird-watchers, hunters, horseback riders, and rockhounds.

No water is available on hiking trails. The range runs from the southwest to the northeast for about twenty-five miles, on the north side of Lanfair Valley.

Amboy Crater: This 285-foot-high cinder cone was formed 6,000 years ago during an eruption that poured hot lava onto Bristol Lake, a dry lake to the south. Not only is it a novelty to climb to the top of the crater, but you're rewarded with terrific views of the twenty-four-square-mile lava field below and to the southwest.

Look for the steep trail climbing the cone's north slope. Allow several hours to hike; the trip takes longer than you'd think. The crater is south of the East Mojave National Scenic Area boundary, south of I-40 off Kelbaker Road, near Amboy.

Cinder Cones And Lava Beds: Some of the thirty cinder cones in this ten-square-mile lava bed are youngsters just 1,000 years old, and some are ancient, up to 5,000 years old. Bring your camera to record the Dali-esque scene: black and red cones, twisted lava tubes, white sand, and black lava flows framed by Joshua trees, cholla, and barrel cactus. The lava beds are about twenty miles east of Baker, off I-15, just north of Kelbaker Road.

Where: In San Bernardino County, north of I-40 and south of I-15 and State 164, and from a point forty-five miles east of Barstow, on the west, to the Nevada border on the east.

Admission: No admission fee to any BLM lands. Museums and state parks have separate entrance fees.

Best time to visit: Spring, followed by fall, and then winter. Summer is usually too hot.

Activities: Desert exploration, rock hunting, amateur geology, hiking, camping, bird-watching, animal identification, mountain biking. Always carry water, emergency supplies, tools, and warm clothing.

Concessions: Very few, and limited mostly to services in small towns like Baker. Bring all your own supplies.

Pets: Allowed on leashes, but better to leave them at home.

For more information:
California Desert Information Center, 831 Barstow Road, Barstow, CA 92311; 619-256-8313.

Providence Mountains State Recreation Area

Providence Mountains State Recreation Area, best known for Mitchell Caverns located on its eastern border, is in the heart of the isolated and sparsely populated East Mojave Desert, eighty miles east of Barstow. The caverns are the main attraction.

The 5,900-acre recreation area, at the east end of the Providence Mountains, is one of the more prominent ranges in the East Mojave. In general, the desert terrain is varied, ranging from dry washes and flat plains to lowland sage, and to pinyon pine and juniper on the mountains' upper slopes.

Elevations range from 4,000 feet at the base of the mountains to 6,000 feet on the crest. Just west of park boundaries the elevation reaches 7,171 feet at the summit of Edgar Peak, an uplifted limestone seabed. The geology of the region is quite complicated; if you're interested, the park headquarters, on a slight rise above the surrounding desert, has pamphlets and books that discuss it in detail.

Though the high elevations tend to moderate temperatures in this park, the summers are still hot. By contrast, Mitchell Caverns—limestone caves beneath the desert floor, formed from an ancient sea that covered the region 250 million years ago— remain at a constant and pleasantly cool 65 degrees year-round.

If you come in August, head straight for the caves, named El Pakiva and Tocopa for two Native American chiefs. The caves are fitted with electric lights; marked paths with railings guide visitors from one area to another past limestone pillars, curtains, stalactites, and stalagmites. According to Ranger John Pelonia, who conducts guided tours, one cavern is young and still in the process of formation, while the other is at the end of its formative life.

When the caves were first discovered years ago, says Pelonia, an opening was tunneled between the two to allow easy

A screech owl at home in the desert

passage. The fresh air sweeping through the tunnel changed the ecology of both caves, drying the newer one and retarding its natural development. After the caves were included in state-park land, rangers installed air-lock doors at both ends of the tunnel to stop the air flow and restore natural conditions. Visitors tour the caves in groups of twenty-five, the exact number of people who fit between the two doors.

Another deep cave, Winding Stair Caverns, is located farther north. Tours of this cave, down steep winding stairs that descend 320 feet below the surface, are restricted to experienced spelunkers.

Above ground, the self-guided Mary Beal Nature Trail loops through the desert for a half mile, aquainting visitors with various desert plants. A longer trail climbs into Crystal Spring Canyon. There are only eight primitive campsites near headquarters, but you can camp anywhere on adjacent BLM land. Bring your own water; the supply at the park is limited.

Where: 100 miles east of Barstow, seventeen miles north of I-40 on Essex Road.

Hours: Dawn to dusk.

Admission: Free to enter the park. Cave tours are $4 for adults, $2 for youths, free for children. Camping is $12 per night, $10 for seniors.

Best time to visit: Spring and fall.

Activities: Cave tours, hiking, camping, self-guided geology field trip.

Concessions: A visitors center.

Pets: Allowed on leashes; $1 extra per night.

For more information:

High Desert Headquarters, P. O. Box 1, Essex, CA 92332; 619-389-2303 or 805-942-0662.

JOSHUA TREE NATIONAL MONUMENT

This 547,790-acre national monument was created in 1936 to protect an abundant forest of Joshua trees, a variety of giant yucca and a member of the agave family. Until recently, some Joshua trees were estimated to be from 300 to 400 years old; botanists now believe the oldest are 700 years old.

The monument is also remarkable for its location on a transition zone between deserts: the high-elevation Mojave Desert in the western half and the Colorado Desert, below 3,000 feet, in the eastern half. The Joshua trees, which grow thickly in the western part of the monument, dwindle away toward the east and are replaced by creosote bush, cholla, and ocotillo.

Of all the desert parks, Joshua Tree is the easiest to reach and the best equipped for recreation, with hiking, nature walks, photography, and rock climbing on the immense boulders that rear up in clusters, punctuating the level desert floor. The campgrounds are also some of the best.

Several of eight campgrounds are located among the boulders; a favorite sport is to kick back in a comfortable chair at a campsite with a pair of binoculars and watch the climbers sweat it out on the vertical granite spires. To tour the park by car, start at the visitors center at the west entrance station, and drive through Lost Horse Valley to Keys View, back to Lost Horse, and then south to the Cottonwood visitors center and the south entrance. The trip takes at least four hours. With a four-wheel-drive, you can explore the park's secondary dirt roads, but vehicles are forbidden to drive off established roads.

More than fifty miles of trails cross the desert, open to hikers, horseback riders, and joggers. Bushwhacking is permitted through the backcountry, where 467,000 acres of roadless desert were recently awarded official wilderness status. Wear high boots as protection against snakes, and carry topographical maps, water, and a compass.

There are five palm oases in Joshua Tree, two at the north and south visitors centers and three at hike-in locations. To hike to Fortynine Palm Oasis, take the 1.5-mile trail at the end of Canyon Road on the monument's northern border—a climb with a 400-foot elevation gain. To hike to Lost Palms Oasis, take the four-mile trail that starts at the Cottonwood visitors center and goes across country.

The monument's longest trail, the thirty-five-mile California Horseback Riding and Hiking Trail, runs from Joshua Lane near Black Canyon at the monument's west end to the north entrance in the center of the park.

The oases are the best places to see wildlife, since these are the only water sources. A list of identified animals includes coyotes, rabbits, bobcats, sidewinders, kangaroo rats, lizards, roadrunners, golden eagles, tarantulas, and burrowing owls.

If rains fall early in the winter, in January and early February, the spring wildflower displays are spectacular in March and early April. When the rains come late, fewer flowers develop and are dominated quickly by weeds.

Seven of eight campgrounds are available on a first-come first-served basis. Black Rock Campground, at 4,000 feet elevation with 100 developed tent and RV sites, can be reserved through MISTIX (800-444-7275). Black Rock and Cottonwood Campgrounds have full facilities and piped water. Six other campgrounds have pit toilets, tables, and fireplaces, but no water.

Where: 140 miles from Los Angeles, between I-10 and State 62. The north entrance and Oasis visitors center are on Utah Trail, in Twentynine Palms. The south entrance and Cottonwood visitors center are off Pinto Basin Road and I-10, twenty-five miles east of Indio.

Hours: Visitors center hours are 8:00 A.M. to 4:30 P.M.

Admission: Entrance fee is $5 per vehicle. $8 – $10 per night to camp at Black Rock and Cottonwood Campgrounds. Six other campgrounds, without water, are free.

Best time to visit: Spring and fall.

Activities: Hiking, camping, horseback riding, rock climbing, desert exploration, interpretive nature walks.

Concessions: There are no restaurants, stores, lodging, or gas stations within Joshua Tree National Monument. Water is available at only four locations – the Oasis visitors center, Indian Cove Ranger Station, Cottonwood Springs, and Blackrock Canyon Campground – so bring your own. Nine campgrounds.

Pets: Allowed on leashes; not allowed on trails.

For more information:

Joshua Tree National Monument, 74485 National Monument Drive, Twentynine Palms, CA 92277; 619-367-7511.

AGUA CALIENTE INDIAN RESERVATION CANYONS

Three large and unusual oases on the Agua Caliente Indian Reservation, on 32,000 acres in Palm Springs, are unique to the low desert and worth a half-day's visit. Palm Canyon, the most widely known of the three, is ten miles long, with more than 3,000 mature native California fan palms, watered by a perennial stream that supports a lush riparian habitat along the creek banks. The oldest of the fan palms, which grow along seven miles of the canyon floor, are estimated at 1,500 to 2,000 years old.

From Palm Springs, follow signs for "Indian Canyons," stop at the reservation entrance to pay a fee, and park in the "Hermit's Bench" parking lot. From here, a trail goes down into the canyon and to the far end, although few visitors hike the entire ten miles. Two to three miles along the trail, by the stream in the shade of the palms, makes a nice trip.

Murray and Andreas Canyons, two adjacent canyons with year-round streams, falls, and pools of water, also begin in the same area. Andreas Canyon's thick palm forests are particularly striking.

An alternative to hiking through the canyons is to take a jeep-safari tour with Desert Off-Road Adventures, which schedules trips between October and May. The one- to four-hour tours let you see more of the canyons in a shorter time than you can on foot.

Where: At the Agua Caliente Indian Reservation on the west side of Palm Springs.
Hours: Daylight hours.
Admission: Entrance fee is $3.50 for adults, $1 for children.
Best time to visit: Spring and early summer.
Activities: Hiking, nature observation, oasis habitat study, driving tours.
Concessions: A snack bar is located on the reservation. For Desert Off-Road Adventures, call 619-324-3378.
Pets: Allowed on leashes.
For more information:
Agua Caliente Indian Reservation, South Palm Canyon Drive, Palm Springs, CA 92263; 619-325-5673.

ANZA-BORREGO DESERT STATE PARK

Anza-Borrego Desert, in a remote valley surrounded by high peaks in eastern San Diego County, is a landscape of contrasts and extremes, where vivid reds and browns stipple the hills and hot sun and deep shade are the norm.

Anza-Borrego is vast. As California's largest state park, with 600,000 acres, it is as big as or bigger than many national parks and forests. That impression is heightened as you explore a few of the park's more accessible sandy washes, twisted rock canyons, weathered cliffs, and palm oases.

For many years few visitors found the valley hospitable enough to live in year-round. Then a community of desert rats and retirees settled near the valley's natural springs, and the town of Borrego Springs grew up. After the park was created, its boundaries were drawn around the town, leaving it an island of private property surrounded by parkland—the only place to eat out, buy groceries and gas, or find supplies.

The park visitors center is just west of town, and in winter, when Borrego Palm Campground is full, the population more than doubles. The town actually has a nice resort hotel and golf course; Borrego Springs thinks of Palm Springs and dreams of glory.

Even in town most of the people you meet are from the outside—campers, hikers, or amateur naturalists. Bird-watching is good, photography is excellent, and, depending on winter rainfall, the spring wildflower displays can be exuberant.

Much is still unknown about Anza-Borrego's most isolated canyons. Recently, archaeologists discovered several early human sites and the fossils of woolly mammoths. Park biologists have identified two new reptile species and found a previously unknown grove of elephant trees in a range called the Santa Monica Mountains.

Native American tribes lived in the valley on and off before the Spanish arrived in 1772 in the person of explorer Pedro Fages. Two years later, Juan Bautista de Anza crossed the desert with a group of colonists from Mexico, on what was to become the Southern Immigrant Trail. In the next century, the Butterfield Overland Stage Line crossed the park on its way to the coast.

Both trails damaged the fragile desert landscape, which has never recovered. The old ruts are still plainly visible from several of the park's paved roads; look for the historic markers indicating the spots.

Any sight-seeing at the park should begin at the visitors center west of Borrego Springs, an energy-efficient underground

Prickly pears

building housing ranger offices, exhibits, and a small theater. A twelve-minute slide show chronicles the change of seasons in the desert, and extensive exhibits explain the area's geology, climate, human history, and flora and fauna.

For a self-guided driving tour, pick up park maps and a tour brochure with numbered points of interest corresponding to the state historical markers located along the park's four main paved roads. The visitors center also has a wide selection of nature books and schedules of park activities, including lectures, nature walks, picnicking, and camping.

You can see a good deal from your car, and even more if you park and take a couple of short nature walks beginning at marked trailheads along the road. Don't explore the interior, where the majority of the roads are soft sand or rock, unless you have a four-wheel-drive vehicle.

Other scenic areas on the driving tour include Carrizo Badlands Overlook; Mountain Palm Springs, an oasis in the Tierra Blanca Mountains; and Font's Point, at the end of a four-mile sandy road, with panoramic views of the valley and the Badlands. (You need a four-wheel-drive to get to the last one.)

The park's single most popular hike starts from Borrego Palm Canyon Campground, at a trailhead a mile from the visitors center. The 1.5-mile walk through the canyon ends at a fertile, shady oasis, where spring waters nurture a stand of native California fan palms. Though palms are ubiquitous in Southern California, only two species are natives.

If you're not staying in the campground, there's a $5 daytime usage fee, which entitles you to enter the campground and drive to the trailhead and to use the showers and other facilities.

Another popular location for hiking, horseback riding, and four-wheel-driving is Coyote Canyon, watered by a year-round stream, about eight miles north of the visitors center. Desert bighorn sheep, protected in Anza-Borrego (and elsewhere in

California) are spotted occasionally in Coyote Canyon, as well as at other park oases, and sometimes even in campgrounds. Park rangers keep up to date on sightings and can point you in the right direction.

Some of our favorite walks are the Elephant Tree Nature Trail, a one-mile path to a couple of lonely elephant trees; Mason Valley Cactus Garden, which bursts into bloom in spring; Culp Valley Overlook, a quarter-mile walk from Culp Valley Campground; and the Yaqui Wells Nature Trail, a two-mile loop starting at Tamarisk Grove Campground.

Although camping is permitted anywhere within the park (at least 200 feet from springs and streams), most people prefer the campgrounds, busy between October and April and deserted in summer. Only two campgrounds, Borrego Palm Canyon and Tamarisk Grove, are developed, with tent and RV sites, hookups, piped water, toilets, showers, tables, and grills. Nine other small campgrounds have some, few, or no facilities. Bring your own water.

Where: Ninety miles east of Escondido on State 78.
Hours: No limit. Visitors center open 9:00 A.M. to 5:00 P.M. from October through May. June through September, weekends and holidays only.
Admission: No entrance fee; $5 per vehicle to enter Borrego Palm Canyon Campground.
Best time to visit: October through May. Summers are like an oven.
Activities: Hiking, camping, four-wheel-drive exploration, desert photography, scenery viewing, plant and animal identification. Carry extra water, food, tools, and emergency supplies.
Concessions: Visitors center and eleven campgrounds are scattered throughout the park. Reservations in developed campgrounds are available through MISTIX (800-444-7275). Primitive campgrounds, with sites issued on a first-come first-served

basis, are free. Groceries, gas, supplies, and restaurants are available in nearby Borrego Springs. Ten other campgrounds are scattered throughout the park.

Pets: Allowed on leashes. Dogs that run loose in the desert may return with a face full of cactus spines. $2 extra fee for pets.

For more Information:

Anza-Borrego Desert State Park, P. O. Box 299, Borrego Springs, CA 92004; 619-767-5311.

SALTON SEA STATE RECREATION AREA and SALTON SEA NATIONAL WILDLIFE REFUGE

The Salton Sea, California's largest man-made lake, was created accidentally in 1905 during the construction of the All American Canal, when the lower Colorado River broke through a dike and flooded the dry, shallow basin between the Chocolate and Santa Rosa Mountains.

But the basin, 278 feet below sea level—the second-lowest spot in the country—was already an ancient seabed; thus it was only a matter of time, geologically speaking, until water found its way back to the area.

It took two years to repair the break and stop the leak, and by that time, the Salton Sea was forty-five miles long, seventeen miles wide, and 100 feet deep in the center, with no outlet. When the Colorado River was returned to its original channel, the sea began to shrink; then irrigation runoff began to drain into the basin, stabilizing the sea and its shoreline.

Today the Whitewater, Alamo, and New Rivers empty into the lake, as do many irrigation canals and small streams, and lake size has been constant at about thirty-five miles long, fifteen miles wide, and ten to fifty feet deep. With no outlet, the water is gradually becoming saltier, with a current salinity of 43,000 parts per million. By comparison, the Pacific Ocean is 35,000 parts per million.

The western shore, a developed recreation area, has several small vacation communities, boat marinas, and private resorts. The 17,868-acre Salton Sea State Recreation Area, on the eastern shore, covers an eighteen-mile-long corridor with camping, boating, fishing, and swimming.

Because the mountain ranges to the west block storms from reaching the basin, the annual rainfall is only three inches. But the climate is hot and humid, especially in summer, when it's one of North America's hottest places. Winter is the time to visit, when temperatures are between seventy and eighty degrees.

Fishing, the main recreation, is good by boat or from the shore. The catch is mostly sargo, corvina, tilapia, and gulf croaker, the only species that thrive in the increasingly salty water. Fishing boats are available for rent.

In 1930, a wildlife refuge was established on the eastern shore for shore birds and waterfowl, and the salt marshes soon became a stopover for migratory birds on the Pacific flyway. The best bird-watching is from Red Hill Marina on the southeast shore, the Wister Waterfowl Area north of Red Hill, the marshes south of the fishing jetty, and Sneaker Beach north of the state recreation area's Headquarters Campground.

A list of 350 birds identified in the refuge includes snow geese, Canada geese, pintail and mallard ducks, green-winged and cinnamon teals, shoveler and ruddy ducks, coots, grebes, egrets, great blue herons, long-billed curlew, willet, godwit, avocet, sandpipers, white pelicans, various swallows, Scott's oriole, and many owls. Ask for a map and a bird list. Bird sightings vary, so check at park headquarters before setting out. Exhibits and a film describe the geology and the natural and human history of the area.

The headquarters also has picnic tables and shade ramadas; a self-guided nature trail goes from here to Mecca Beach Campground. Campfire programs are held year-round. Five campgrounds in the recreation area are open to tents and RVs, with varying facilities; all have water, tables, some shade, toilets and swimming areas. Mecca Campground has the best swimming beach and showers to wash off the salt water. Some sites have hookups.

Where: In Imperial County, between State 86 and State 111 north of Brawley and El Centro.

Hours: No limit.

Admission: No entrance fee for the state park. Camping fees vary.

Best time to visit: Fall, winter, and spring.

Activities: Fishing, camping, bird-watching. The Salton Sea's water is murky but clean. The salt may make your eyes or open cuts sting.

Concessions: Campground reservation through MISTIX (800-444-7275). Groceries, supplies, and bait and tackle sold.

Pets: Allowed on leashes.

For more information:

Salton Sea Recreation Area, P. O. Box 3166, North Shore, CA 92254; 619-393-3052.

PICACHO STATE RECREATION AREA

Most of us know the mighty Colorado River as it runs through the Grand Canyon—a torrent swollen by tributaries, carver of one of the seven wonders of the modern world.

But there's another aspect to the Colorado: the river as a tamed giant, a lazy creature trapped between downstream dams, winding its way in wide loops toward the Mexican border and the Sea of Cortez.

After the dams were built, to provide drinking water and irrigation for the parched Southwest, this other Colorado River, full of water year-round, became an important wintering ground and nesting site for migratory birds and a recreation area for fishermen, boaters, waterskiers and bird-watchers.

Picacho State Recreation Area, a desert park along eight miles of the lower Colorado River near the Mexican and Arizona borders, protects 4,880 acres of wetlands and marsh and the surrounding desert hills, a mixed habitat that supports a wide range of wildlife.

From the campground and marina, fishermen and boaters have access to fifty-five miles of open river between Parker Dam upstream and Imperial Dam fifteen miles downstream. There's enough current along this stretch for river rafting, but not too much for canoeists trying to paddle upstream. Waterskiing is also permitted within the recreation-area boundaries, one of few places on the lower Colorado where it's allowed.

If you have a boat you can go into Adobe, Taylor, and Island Lakes in the recreation area, and Ferguson and Martinez Lakes downstream—all big backwater lakes with extensive tule marshes, created by Imperial Dam. Both birds and marine life thrive here, and the fishing is good. Bass bite year-round, crappie bite in late winter and early spring, and channel and flathead catfish bite in late spring and early fall.

Bird photography is excellent within the tule marshes; bring a telephoto lens and fast film for close-ups. Other good locations are at points along the river banks, where you can set a tripod and/or a blind.

The ranger station's list of sighted birds includes swallows, sparrows, towhees, roadrunners, cactus wrens, white-winged doves, buzzards, and red-tailed hawks; migratory birds commonly seen during the winter months include snowy egrets, ducks, snow geese, cormorants, blue herons, and ibis.

Plant life also thrives along the river, with Carrizo cane, tule marsh, palo verde trees, desert ironwood, cottonwood trees, mesquite, and cactus, but these indigenous species are threatened by fast-growing, greedy tamarisk trees—an African import that hoards available water and crowds out native habitat. A program is under way to remove the tamarisk.

Hiking trails explore the arid hills west of the river, where a small herd of endangered desert bighorn sheep live on isolated ridges. With binoculars you may glimpse them on the skyline. Their main enemy isn't man but a population of feral burros, which were brought here during the gold rush. Like the tamarisk trees, the burros monopolize waterholes and pasturage. Efforts to move or shoot them have been stopped by animal-rights groups.

Other animals in the park include rabbits, coyotes, bobcats, raccoons, striped skunks, mule deer, ground squirrels, and, more rarely, muskrats and beavers.

Gold was discovered at Picacho in the late 1800s, and by 1904 the town had a population of 2,500. After the dams were built, the town was flooded and is now under water. The mill, a historic site, survived on high ground near park headquarters.

The best time to visit Picacho is between November and mid-April, when temperatures are mild. The wildflowers begin blooming in February, and bird-watching is good starting in November. Picacho is virtually deserted in summer. Daytime temperatures often reach 120 degrees, and after April the mosquitoes are thick. If you must come during these months, bring DEET-based insect repellent and protective clothing.

Headquarters Campground, near the ranger station, has fifty sites and piped drinking water. Several "boat-in" camp-grounds with launch ramps are upriver from headquarters. Hiking trails and four-wheel-drive tracks go through the back-country.

To get to Picacho State Recreation Area from Winterhaven, take Picacho Road, paved for the first six miles and graded gravel for the next eighteen miles. A rougher route, Hyduke Mine Road, goes to the park from County S34. During rains or thunderstorms, watch for flash floods.

Where: Twenty-four miles directly north of Winterhaven, across the border from Yuma, Arizona.

Hours: No limit.

Admission: No entrance fee. Fees for overnight camping; make reservations through MISTIX (800-444-7275).

Best time to visit: November through mid-April.

Activities: Camping, fishing, canoeing, boating, desert hiking, bird-watching, photography. All campfires must be in fire rings.

Concessions: The ranger station has a small visitors center. Bring your own food, supplies, and firewood. No telephones.

Pets: Allowed on leashes.

For more information:

Picacho State Recreation Area, P. O. Box 1207, Winterhaven, CA 92283; 619-393-3052.

CIBOLA AND IMPERIAL
NATIONAL WILDLIFE REFUGES

If you're a bird-watcher, consider visiting one of several national wildlife refuges located on both sides of the Colorado River, north of Picacho State Recreation Area. The Cibola Refuge is to the north, accessible on dirt roads off State 78.

Drive along the road until you find a good viewpoint close to the water. The refuge headquarters is on the Arizona side of the river; cross the river just south of Palo Verde County Park. You can also stay overnight here. The park has a campground with twenty-five tent and RV sites; no fees to camp. The Imperial National Wildlife Refuge is to the south, just upstream from Imperial Dam; wildlife viewing here is possible from dirt roads off County S24 out of Winterhaven. Look for visitor parking and concessions on the California side of the river.

Where: On the Colorado River south of Blythe.

Hours: No limit.

Admission: No entrance fees. Fees for overnight camping.

Best time to visit: November through mid-April.

Activities: Camping, fishing, canoeing, boating, desert hiking, bird-watching, photography.

Concessions: In nearby towns.

For more information:

Cibola National Wildlife Refuge, P. O. Box AP, Blythe, CA 92225; 714-922-2129.

Imperial National Wildlife Refuge, P. O. Box 2217, Martinez Lake, AZ 85364; 602-783-3400

Index

Other titles in the Natural Wonders / Green Guides series:

Natural Wonders of Alaska
Natural Wonders of Florida
Green Guide to Hawaii
Natural Wonders of Idaho
Natural Wonders of Maine
Natural Wonders of Massachusetts
Natural Wonders of New Hampshire
Natural Wonders of New Jersey
Natural Wonders of Ohio
Green Guide to Oregon
Natural Wonders of Southern California
Natural Wonders of Virginia
Green Guide to Washington

All books are $9.95 at bookstores.
Or order directly from the publisher (add $3.00 shipping and
handling for direct orders):

Country Roads Press
P.O. Box 286
Castine, Maine 04421
Toll-free phone number: **800-729-9179**